DIGITAL RESILIENCE

Is Your Company Ready for the Next Cyber Threat?

RAY A. ROTHROCK

Foreword by Richard A. Clarke

AMACOM
American Management Association

New York • Atlanta • Brussels • Chicago • Mexico City • San Francisco
Shanghai • Tokyo • Toronto • Washington, D.C.

To my wife, Meredith, whose love, encouragement, and support makes this book possible in countless ways. And to my son, Nathaniel, the finest friend a man could have.

Bulk discounts available. For details visit:
www.amacombooks.org/go/specialsales
Or contact special sales:
Phone: 800-250-5308
Email: specialsls@amanet.org
View all the AMACOM titles at: www.amacombooks.org
American Management Association: www.amanet.org

Library of Congress Cataloging-in-Publication Data

Names: Rothrock, Ray A., author.
Title: Digital resilience : is your company ready for the next cyber threat? / by Ray A. Rothrock.
Description: New York : American Management Association, [2018] | Includes bibliographical references and index.
Identifiers: LCCN 2017051458 (print) | LCCN 2017055762 (ebook) | ISBN 9780814439258 (ebook) | ISBN 9780814439241 (hardcover : alk. paper)
Subjects: LCSH: Computer networks–Security measures. | Computer security.
Classification: LCC TK5105.59 (ebook) | LCC TK5105.59 .R685 2018 (print) | DDC 658.4/78–dc23
LC record available at https://lccn.loc.gov/2017051458

About AMA
American Management Association (www.amanet.org) is a world leader in talent development, advancing the skills of individuals to drive business success. Our mission is to support the goals of individuals and organizations through a complete range of products and services, including classroom and virtual seminars, webcasts, webinars, podcasts, conferences, corporate and government solutions, business books, and research. AMA's approach to improving performance combines experiential learning—learning through doing—with opportunities for ongoing professional growth at every step of one's career journey.

10 9 8 7 6 5 4 3 2 1

CONTENTS

FOREWORD

The White House, Pentagon, State Department, NSA, an Iranian nuclear plant unconnected to the Internet, and numerous large banks and corporations have been successfully hacked. Almost any network can be.

The goal of network owners and operators should not be just to prevent unauthorized penetration. That goal is almost too ambitious to be realized. In addition to seeking to exclude malicious actors, network operators should seek a more attainable goal, to be resilient under attack. Resilient networks are those that quickly identify and limit the activities of unauthorized actors. They are networks that are architected to minimize the potential for damage. Most important, they are characterized by an ability to resume essential operations quickly after sustaining a disabling attack. As cyber threats become more persistent, more sophisticated, and more pernicious, we must take a proactive approach to achieving this digital resilience. Making this pursuit more difficult, the topography of the threat landscape is becoming increasingly diverse and complex, with new and unique malware popping up every day.

On May 12, 2017, at 7:44 a.m. UTC, a lone computer in Southeast Asia had its contents encrypted by the WannaCry ransomware. Thirty minutes later, WannaCry had reached Latin America, and by 10:05 a.m., the malware had its first victims in Europe. Within a single day, it had infected over 230,000 computers globally, but was stopped in its tracks two days later by a cybersecurity researcher who discovered a kill switch in the WannaCry code. In this very brief period of time, countless major organizations and multinational firms had their operations interrupted, perhaps the most notable of which were a few hospitals of the U.K.'s National Health Service. They were forced to turn away patients as their MRI machines and other equipment were rendered inoperable, thus showing the world a mechanism whereby computer code may indirectly lead to the deaths of innocent civilians.

WannaCry could have been far worse, had it not been for the kill switch that was hidden away in the code, and the cybersecurity community is already bracing for the next iteration of a similar ransomware that doesn't include one. This particular attack was indiscriminate in that it infected any device that was vulnerable; however, large firms with valuable information are now being increasingly targeted with advanced attacks that are tailored to their unique systems (see Chapter 1 for the Target cyberattack, circa 2013). These attacks—although less pervasive—are much more effective and invite a more comprehensive approach to cybersecurity. Companies need to be resilient and adapt, because at some point, they *will* have to recover from one. It is not a question of if, but when.

The fundamental truth that C-suite executives must acknowledge in today's digital ecosystem is that no company, no organization, and no network is impenetrable. We must view our efforts toward engineering networks with the assumption that—to some extent—*they* will get in and attempt to acquire what they want. It's up to the cybersecurity professionals to allow this assumption to inform their network design, and shape subsequent decisions around what cybersecurity tools are eventually implemented. In this way, it's critical to understand that a dollar spent on efforts to preemptively mitigate the damage is money better spent than a dollar spent trying to prevent network penetration altogether.

Companies often focus far too much on prevention, rather than, for instance, malware containment or implementing robust means of data recovery. I believe much of these misguided efforts can be attributed to a lack of cybersecurity understanding in the board room. Even today, after numerous high-profile attacks have received extensive news coverage, one would think that the issue is sufficiently salient for every firm to take concrete steps toward protecting itself. Yet, it seems that many board members of major companies are painfully unaware of the importance of securing their networks, or of the risks and costs—both tangible and intangible—that are realized after a cyberattack. Companies may lose their customers' trust, diminish their brand's image, or incur costs that significantly reduce their bottom line. These ramifications can even affect mergers and acquisitions. For example, in 2016 a massive data breach caused a $350 million decrease in Yahoo's selling price to Verizon. Our job as practitioners in the industry is to explain these issues to the decision makers in a clear manner to cultivate a common understanding of digital resilience and its importance.

Cybersecurity must also increasingly be seen as an integral part of the business strategy of today's firms, as a breach has a substantial financial impact on the business that may prevent it from achieving its other goals. Whether it's legal costs to compensate customers for having their personal information stolen, or foregone revenue of products you didn't sell because the schematics were stolen and the product copied elsewhere, a data breach can be far more expensive than people generally realize. Too often security is viewed as something peripheral to the organization, but we must all make an effort to bring it into the fold, under the umbrella of the C-suite. Our security professionals must have a seat at the table, because a significant portion of the business's continued success rides on their performance.

This book discusses one of the most important issues of our time, and it will only become increasingly important as time goes on. Ray outlines the challenges of cybersecurity with a litany of real-world examples of high-profile attacks, looking at what each organization got right, and what they got wrong. However, what I like most about this book is the explanation of technical topics in a manner accessible to the average person who has no background in the fundamentals of computer science or network engineering. By describing these different systems and issues in "plain English," Ray is increasing the common person's fluency of cyberspace discourse, which will certainly help the industry as-a-whole down the road. It's imperative that the public develops an educational foundation of what all of this means, so that a cyberattack is no longer viewed as an enigmatic occurrence that only affects people other than oneself.

By reading this book, you'll develop a much greater understanding of the nature of these issues. You'll learn what digital resiliency is, and how to create it. You'll learn the technical fundamentals of networks, how they operate, and why the distributed nature of the Internet leaves so many networks vulnerable to attack. You'll also grasp the true inevitability of a successful attack on your own network and learn why it's so important to prepare yourself for that moment. Most important, Ray delineates many different actions that you can take today to implement safeguards for different threats. He illuminates specific actionable items to employ in the workplace and board room, and describes how these actions can instill a better sense of cyber risk among the decision makers at your firm.

America proved after Pearl Harbor, after the launch of Sputnik, and following 9/11 that it was a resilient nation. Unfortunately, today America's networks are not resilient. This important book, written by one of the nation's most recognized experts in cybersecurity, is about how we can make America's networks, and those of others, resilient in the face of the inevitable attack that succeeds in penetrating the porous perimeter. As I said in my book, *Cyber War*, in 2010, cyberspace is the new frontier, within which the wars of the future will be fought. Whether between nation-states, or between private-sector companies and hackers, the effects of ongoing campaigns in this theater will reverberate throughout all of society, eventually affecting us all. In this new reality, digital resilience means survival.

Richard A. Clarke

1

INTENSIVELY NETWORKED

Why Resilience Is the Only Rational Cybersecurity Choice

November 30, 2013—From offices in Bangalore, India, employees of the Silicon Valley security firm FireEye alerted Minneapolis-based Target that they had detected evidence of a security breach of Target's digital network. By this time the U.S. retailer, second only to Walmart in size, had been a FireEye client for about six months, having hired the company for $1.6 million to create a state-of-the-art network security system.[1]

The 2013 attack against Target was one of more than three thousand that year.[2] So, cyberattacks are far from unusual. In fact in 2016, the Ponemon Institute, which conducts independent research on privacy, data protection, and information security policy, looked at the "likelihood of a company having one or more data breach occurrences in the next twenty-four months" and concluded that each of the 383 companies it surveyed had a "26 percent probability of a material data breach involving ten thousand lost or stolen records."[3] Put another way, over the long term, the nature of the threat against the digital network of your business is defined by two facts.

- Number one, breaches are, by their nature, highly probable occurrences—so probable that, over the long term, they can be deemed inevitable. Breaches will happen. Breaches will happen to you.
- Number two, breaches are, by their nature, costly in time, worry, and reputation.

ANSWERING THE CALL TO ACTION

The call to action is clear: We must protect ourselves and our enterprises. The problem is that no means of protection is bulletproof. It is not enough to erect a "firewall" around the firm's digital infrastructure, issue antimalware software to all hands, pronounce your enterprise "secure," and walk away. Such passive, static security measures are necessary, but they are not sufficient. In Chapter 3, we will review the most effective and cost-effective strategies and devices for "securing" our networks. We must note now, however, and always bear in mind that security alone offers no silver bullet. All security approaches are inherently and inevitably flawed because the vulnerabilities of digital connection are inherent and inevitable. They are the price of opening ourselves to the opportunities of connection. Once we accept the risk-reward trade-off of digital connectivity, our next step is to survive—and even thrive—under attack. Digital security is an incomplete answer. Digital resilience completes the answer.

As a concept, digital resilience is relatively new—but only because digital technology is relatively new, and networked digital technology is even newer. The fact is that *digital* resilience is a subset of *resilience*, which is a characteristic of biological, ecological, social, national, and institutional systems that have survived and thrived, some of them since time immemorial. Whereas digital security is about security, digital resilience is about how you do business in today's intensively interconnected environment. It is not confined to the realm of IT specialists, but is a whole-business strategy.

THE TARGET ATTACK: WHAT A FAILURE OF RESILIENCE LOOKS LIKE

Only two things make the 2013 attack on Target unusual: its magnitude—70 million customers became victims—and the amount and detail of insight we have gained from it. (While the Equifax data breach, which took place during May–July 2017 but was not reported until September 2017, affected at least twice as many victims—145.5 million American consumers, close to half the U.S. population—we don't as yet have sufficient information to create a definitively illuminating narrative.) The Target attack reveals the severe limits of conventional digital security. More important, it is a call to move beyond these limits. The numbers make it clear that attack is virtually inevitable. We need something more than the current "state of the art" in digital security.

It is true that most private- and public-sector leaders agree on the necessity of making preparations for survival under cyberattack. All sophisticated businesses have active disaster recovery plans (DRP) and business continuity plans (BCP). They understand that having an emergency plan for a crisis is essential. But both DRPs and BCPs are very different from a cyber recovery plan. The purpose of this book is to persuade managers, C-suite executives, and boards of directors that the default environment in which their highly connected businesses, institutions, and government agencies operate is in crisis. Connectivity creates both frictionless business opportunity and frictionless vulnerability to attack. This is today's default situation. Mere survival is not a sufficiently ambitious objective. Intensively connected enterprises need to *thrive* in high-risk environments and even under attack.

Thriving under attack is not a radical proposal. It is a function of digital resilience. As defined very ably by Andrew Zolli and Ann Marie Healy, resilience is "the capacity of a system, enterprise, or a person to maintain its core purpose and integrity in the face of dramatically changed circumstances."[4] The chapters that follow are about applying the concept and quality of resilience specifically to digital networks. Before we get to these chapters, however, let us take a close-up look at what happened to a network whose operators failed to make it resilient. The Target attack, breach, and data theft, one of about three thousand that year, is representative of today's digital business environment. It is also an event about which we have an abundance of information.

ACTION ITEM

There is no bulletproof protection against cyberattack. Digital security is mandatory but not sufficient. In addition to digital security, understand, embrace, and implement digital resilience as a strategy for surviving and thriving in an inherently insecure digital environment.

On March 26, 2014, John Mulligan, executive vice president and chief financial officer of Target Corporation, testified before the Senate Committee on Commerce, Science, & Transportation. His unenviable task was to explain why and how the credit card data of 40 million of his company's customers had been stolen. "It appears that intruders entered our system on November 12[, 2013]," he testified. "With the benefit of hindsight and new information, we are now asking hard questions regarding the judgments that were made at that time and assessing whether different judgments may have led to different outcomes."[5]

Without doubt, the first "hard question" is why, having been alerted by Bangalore on November 30, 2013, Target's Minneapolis-based Security Operations Center did exactly nothing. Nothing. The next question is, why, after a second alert was sent on December 2, they also did nothing.[6] Target did not even begin an "internal investigation" until December 12, when the retailer was "notified by the Justice Department of suspicious activity involving payment cards used at Target stores." Target personnel met with the DOJ and the Secret Service on December 13, hired "an outside team of experts to lead a thorough forensic investigation" on December 14, and on December 15 "confirmed that criminals had infiltrated our system, installed malware on our point-of-sale network and potentially stolen guest payment card data. That same day, we removed the malware from virtually all registers in our U.S. stores."[7]

By this time, records affecting 70 million customers had been stolen: data for 40 million debit and credit cards plus the personally identifiable information (PII) of those customers in addition to 30 million others whose credit card data was not stolen.

For 40 to 70 million Target customers, there were the ugly consequences of identity theft—unauthorized charges to sort out, inability to access credit, endless phone calls to credit reporting agencies, getting blindsided by fraudulent credit and loan applications, and no way to know when and where the ripples created by compromised PII would end.

For Target, the gross expense created by the breach during 2013–2014 was reported as $252 million. Insurance compensation reduced this to $162 million, and tax deductions brought it down to $105 million.[8] Nevertheless, the company's profits fell 46 percent in its fourth fiscal quarter of 2013 and were down by more than a third for all of 2013.[9] More than 140 lawsuits from customers and financial institutions rolled in. In March 2015, Target settled a class-action suit brought by customers for $10 million; in August, Target settled with Visa for $67 million; and in December, the company settled with several banks (whose credit cards were compromised) for $39 million in damages.[10] Both Target CIO Beth Jacob and CEO Gregg Steinhafel resigned following the breach.[11] Federal and state authorities have threatened fines and other penalties.[12] Beyond all of this, there was the damage to the Target brand and reputation, a hit difficult to measure.

"We are asking hard questions about whether we could have taken different actions before the breach was discovered that would have resulted in different outcomes," Mulligan told the senators. "In particular, we are focused on what information we had that could have alerted us to the breach earlier. . . ."[13]

There is an answer to this. An earlier alert would have made no difference. Two reasons: First, Target made no response to the two alerts it did receive. There is no compelling reason to believe it would have responded to an alert received earlier. Second, the November 30 alert came *after* the network had been infiltrated but *before* data was being exfiltrated. The theft itself started on December 2, the date of the second alert. Nurtured on pop culture images of "wired-in" cyber prodigies gone over to the dark side, the uninformed picture "hackers" as superhuman geniuses and assume they move with infinite stealth and at great speed. Those who possess even basic knowledge of the complexity of large digital networks, however, know that infiltrating a network, finding what you want to take, and then exfiltrating that material—which typically amounts to huge quantities of data—takes time: days, weeks, sometimes months.

As far as can be determined, exfiltration from Target did not begin until December 2 and continued for nearly two weeks. The process was painstaking: The malware automatically sent data to three different U.S.-based staging points, servers located in Ashburn, Virginia, Provo, Utah, and Los Angeles, California, active only between 10:00 a.m. and 6:00 p.m. Central Standard Time, probably to reduce the chances that the outflow would be detected by burying it in the massive volume of normal workday traffic. From the U.S. staging points, the data was sent to vpsville.ru, a Moscow-based webhosting service, which operates openly. The company's spokesman, Alexander Kiva, later unapologetically explained that the company has far too many clients to effectively monitor.[14]

ADVANCED PERSISTENT THREAT: THE ENEMY WITHIN

Far from being smash-and-grab affairs, most meaningful breaches take time. Indeed, an entire category of breach is categorized as an "Advanced Persistent Threat" (APT), a network attack in which the intruder not only gains access to the network but remains active in it for a long period of time. To date, the most spectacular documented APT was that of "APT1," which was exposed in a February 2013 report by the Mandiant security company. "APT1 is believed to be the 2nd Bureau of [China's] People's Liberation Army (PLA) General Staff Department's (GSD) 3rd Department. . . ." Since 2006, APT1 compromised "141 companies spanning 20 major industries," most of them U.S.-based. It "maintained access to victim networks for an average of 356 days." The longest span was 1,764 days of continuous network access—four years and ten months."[15]

ACTION ITEM

Truly destructive network breaches are not smash-and-grab "attacks." A successful breach is better described and understood as a chronic infection rather than a transitory attack, as espionage and embezzlement rather than burglary, as an invasion and occupation rather than a hit-and-run raid. An intruder can live and operate in your network for hours, days, weeks, years. Detecting and neutralizing a breach begins by gaining complete and comprehensive knowledge of your networks and their connections. Take steps to get this knowledge.

On the one hand, the persistence of the Advanced Persistent Threat is truly appalling. On the other hand, the takeaway lesson of the APT is that the most serious and destructive attacks provide us with a great deal of time to discover them—*if* we pay attention and *if* we know our own networks both comprehensively and intimately. But few enterprises pay enough attention, and even fewer know much of anything about the networks they operate.

APT1 was a highly crafted military operation backed by the resources of the government of the world's most populous nation. As for the level of skill required to pull off the Target breach, however, Jim Walter, director of threat intelligence operations at the McAfee security firm, called the malware that was used "absolutely unsophisticated and uninteresting."[16] Two of its main moving parts were off-the-shelf malware, Citadel and Kaptoxa (pronounced kap-TOE-sha), both available for purchase on underground (or undergroundish) websites well known to cybercriminals. The first was used to steal credentials enabling the attackers to enter the Target system. The second was used to steal credit card information of customers who swiped their cards at the stores' cash registers.[17] Both APT1 and the Target breach were long present in the networks they attacked. The significance of this is that they were discoverable, if the operators of the networks under attack had possessed better, fuller knowledge of those networks.

ANATOMY OF A "RUN-OF-THE-MILL" EXPLOIT

Although spectacularly successful, the Target breach was a run-of-the-mill cyber exploit. That means two things. First, it was containable, if not stoppable—which is true of the vast majority of cyberattacks. Second, it was the kind of attack likely to hit anyone who runs any digitally connected business—in other words, anyone who runs just about any business today. Using research from Aorato Labs and the SANS Institute, we can actually trace the likely steps the attackers took.[18] It is worth tracing because some variation of the Target attack has likely been, is being, or will be aimed at your business.

Casing the caper. Retail companies deal with retail customers, but they also interact with an array of B2B vendors. Often, these vendors are given privileged access to networks and data, especially for bidding and billing purposes. A simple Google search would have revealed to the attackers a wealth of information about Target's vendors. Among these was Fazio Mechanical, a Sharpsburg, Pennsylvania–based refrigeration systems contractor that frequently served Target. Additional research could also have turned up, on a Microsoft website, a case study describing how Target used Microsoft System Center

Configuration Manager (SCCM) to automatically update and security-patch much of its software infrastructure, including the software for its POS (point-of-sale) system—the system communicating with its retail checkout counter card readers.

Without so much as having to glance away from their computer monitors or committing any crime, the attackers could have, first, found a means of hijacking the credentials that would get them into Target's network and, second, obtained a remarkably detailed picture of the retailer's POS system.

Phishing for an entrance. The attackers launched an email phishing attack against Target's vendors, such as Fazio Mechanical, which were likely to have privileged access to Target's network. A phishing email masquerades as a message from some trusted entity—a bank, for example—and may trick the recipient into revealing confidential information or clicking on a seemingly legitimate attachment that executes an invasion. In the Target case, someone at Fazio innocently clicked on an email attachment that opened a malware program, which infected Fazio's network and the computers on it. Against Fazio, it is thought that the Target attackers used Citadel, an off-the-shelf password-stealing bot developed by cybercriminals from an older item of malware called ZeuS. A Trojan horse used to invade a computer by duping the victim into opening an attachment, ZeuS surfaced in 2007. Both Citadel and ZeuS are available for sale on black market hacker websites.

Stealing credentials. Having obtained from Fazio the credentials needed to enter Target's network via a vendor portal, the attackers let themselves in. One of the things you need to know about your network is that it is only as secure as the networks with which it connects. Vulnerability in a *vendor's* network can bring *you* down. What Target didn't know about its network included what it didn't know about its vendors' networks.

Gaining access. Because Fazio Mechanical bid and billed Target electronically, it was connected to Target's Ariba billing system web application;[19] to Partners Online, Target's project management and contract submissions system;[20] and to a Property Development Zone web app. None of these was a wide-open *front door* to Target's systems, but the connections enabled the attackers to upload a nefarious script called a *web shell,* which is a *back door* through which the attackers could both upload files and execute high-level operating system commands within Target's system.

Finding the money. As any burglar knows, getting in is only half the heist. Once inside, you have to find the merchandise. With access to Target's operating system, the intruders were able to search the Active Directory. What they were looking for were databases relating to credit/debit cards. Ultimately, these consisted both of files with customers' personally identifiable information (PII) and files relating to POS devices, the card readers at the checkout counters. Having identified these two targets in the Active Directory, the attackers were able to obtain the IP addresses needed to access both the PII files (turned out there were about 70 million of them) and the POS devices.

Getting the privileges. Possessing the necessary IP addresses is not sufficient to get you into those addresses. The attackers needed Domain Admin privileges, which they obtained (it is believed) by using a technique that is familiar to hackers, "Pass-the-Hash." When a legitimate Admin logs into the Active Directory using her credentials, a Windows computer generates a token called an "NT hash." The token, which replaces the user's password, lives in the computer's memory and vanishes when the computer is rebooted. But servers are rarely rebooted, and so valid NT hash tokens litter the system's memory. An attacker simply needs to dig into the machine memory in order to "pass the hash" and thereby obtain Admin privileges.

Opening a new account. With Domain Admin privileges in hand, the attackers were now empowered to create their very own Domain Admin account, just as if they were trusted Target employees—at least as long as the legitimate Admin, whose token they had purloined, did not change her password. Passwords, the intruders knew, are not frequently changed. The attackers made up a user name, "best1_user," which looked a lot like any existing legitimate user name. No one at Target red-flagged it, and "best1_user" served the attackers for more than two months, plenty long enough to infiltrate the Target system, to probe it, and to commandeer the computers they needed in order to exfiltrate the credit card data they were after.

Overcoming last-ditch network defenses. Even though Target's Minneapolis-based security team had failed—twice—to act on the warnings it received, the company's network was hardly defenseless. There were firewalls as well as other good security measures that remained obstacles to access and to infiltration, let alone to the exfiltration of masses of data.

Getting around a firewall? As it turns out, there's an app for that. It is off-the-shelf, perfectly legitimate, and *openly* available online. Called Angry IP Scanner, it is billed as a "fast and friendly network scanner," requires no installation, can be copied, and can be used anywhere. It pings a network's IP addresses to see which ones are alive and, if the user wishes, it will resolve all the necessary network information—host name, MAC address, ports, and much more.[21] Using this information, the attackers employed an innocuous port-forwarding utility to circumvent firewall rules. They did not break through the firewall, they tunneled under it.

Having defeated the firewall, the attackers used standard Microsoft Windows network utilities (PsExec and a Remote Desktop Protocol tool) to enable the remote running of processes on various Target machines. They also made use of another Microsoft program, Orchestrator, a workflow management tool that allows IT managers to automate creation, monitoring, and deployment of resources across a company's systems.[22] Orchestrator not only gave the attackers the look of legitimate users, it established the "persistence" of access that gave the intruders time to infiltrate the system, identify and take what they wanted, and then exfiltrate these masses of data.

Getting the PII. The first files exfiltrated were those containing the PII of 70 million Target customers. But this wasn't the loot the attackers were after. They wanted the credit cards—the data they could sell to *their* customers, who would use it to clone cards *Target's* customers had swiped at Target cash registers. Because Target adhered to the Payment Card Industry Data Security Standard (PCI DSS), credit card details were not available in the same files or even on the same servers that held the PII data. PCI compliance could not prevent the breach, but it did delay the attackers. Had they been less focused, the intruders might have given up after having "merely" stolen the identities of some 70 million human beings.

Installing Kaptoxa. Having discovered that they could not extract usable credit card information from the PII data, the attackers turned next to their off-the-shelf Kaptoxa malware, which is memory-scraping software uploaded into POS devices (checkout counter credit card readers) to capture credit and debit card data.[23]

Pretty slick. The only catch is that Kaptoxa needed to be *installed* on Target's POS devices. The attackers therefore had to turn back to hijacking more devices—this time exploiting the network connections between the relevant computers in Target's system and the POS devices. Doing this enabled the attackers to install Kaptoxa.

Exfiltrating. Even though PCI-compliant merchants like Target encrypt credit card data at the point of sale, most POS devices very briefly store the data—unencrypted—in local RAM (random access memory). Kaptoxa exploits this fleeting exposure to copy the unencrypted data from a card as it is swiped. The malware then stores that data in free RAM in the POS device. The attackers needed to set up a means of moving the data from this short-term parking to a remote server, from which the aggregated data could ultimately be uploaded to the servers of vpsville.ru, the Moscow-based webhosting service the attackers used. They employed three U.S.-based servers to exfiltrate data from Target's POS devices. This was a multistage process carried out incrementally over nearly two weeks. Once on the U.S. servers, however, the data was quickly sent to vpsville.ru.

CYBERCRIME AS CYBERCOMPETITION

The attackers now had the PII of some 70 million customers and the credit card data of 40 million of those customers. What would they do with it? Brian Krebs, one of the nation's foremost reporters on cybercrime, found out by focusing on the end product of the breach rather than how it began.[24]

In December 2013, several banks, most of them small, asked Krebs to investigate a sudden off-the-charts spike in fraud rates using credit cards from their institutions. Krebs logged onto a website, well-known in the fraudster community, that sells stolen credit cards. The site announced having received a huge shipment of cards. Krebs quickly matched the bank identification numbers (BINs) of the advertised cards with cards issued by the banks who had engaged him. He took this information to the banks and told them how they could go to the website and use Bitcoins (a currency often used for illicit online transaction because it is both untraceable and unrecoverable) to buy some of the cards back. He then asked the banks to determine if the cards had a common point of purchase. The banks reported that all the cards had been used at Target between Thanksgiving and December 15, 2013.

With this discovery, the plot unraveled. Card shops—also called dumps shops—operate on the web much like any other online business. The biggest difference is that the merchandise they offer is, exclusively, stolen. They present their merchandise in a customer-friendly manner, for example, allowing buyers to select by BIN, type of card (MasterCard, Visa, and so on), expiration date, country, and name of issuing financial institution. They don't sell cards physically stolen from banks or stores. They sell the data copied from those cards. Theirs is a 100 percent online business. Purchasers click on their desired dumps, download the data from the shop, and then use it either to clone their own physical cards or to make purchases online without a physical card.[25]

Let's ponder this a moment.

First: Without question, the attackers are criminals, but they operate like ordinary businesspeople. Most of the tools of their trade are purchased off-the-shelf, and they run their criminal enterprises pretty much as they would run any lawful business.

Second: The attackers are either partners with or wholesalers to online sellers of stolen credit card data. The online storefronts they supply use brand names, create graphical logos, make promises to their customers, and even offer money-back guarantees. They are international criminal enterprises, without question, yet in many ways they behave like legitimate retail businesses. These cybercriminals did not simply rob Target and victimize its customers, they *competed with* the credit card companies, the banks, and the credit card holders. Target, like other targets of criminal cyber breaches, discovered that it was operating not only in a business environment made hostile by rogue "hackers," but in a business environment inhabited by particularly aggressive and vicious *competitors.*

ACTION ITEM

The law accurately brands cyberattacks as crimes and the attackers as criminals. Business leaders, however, may be better served by thinking of the attackers as especially ruthless and unethical competitors. Mounting and maintaining an aggressive defense against them requires more than cyber-*security* measures. It requires *business* measures—decisions and policies that involve the entire enterprise. Digital resilience is a whole-business strategy.

And there is even more. Analysis of the code uploaded to Target's system turned up the name Rescator, the alias of a hacker who was also the proprietor of a dumps shop operating out of the Black Sea port city of Odessa, Ukraine. Krebs discovered that Rescator had also gone by the name Helkern, which was the alias of an Odessan (twenty-two years old in 2013) named Andrey Khodyrevskiy. While the evidence is strong that Rescator and Helkern/Khodyrevskiy are one and the same person, it is not definitive.[26] That Khodyrevskiy is a hacker is certain, and that he operates out of Ukraine is hardly surprising. Both Ukraine and Russia are notorious sources and centers of global cybercrime. As the attacks on the 2015–2016 U.S. presidential campaign and election process, including the hacking of the Democratic National Convention, demonstrate, much of this crime is intimately tied to the Russian government.[27]

GETTING A HANDLE ON OUR NETWORKS

As individuals and as businesses, we rely on our digital networks to enable and amplify our greatest strengths. Even as they do this, however, they simultaneously enable and amplify our most dangerous vulnerabilities. Digitally enhanced connectivity is the mother of all double-edged swords. It opens us to unprecedented levels of opportunity and exposes us to equally unprecedented levels of risk. Were it not for digital networks, Target Corporation would likely consist of no more than a handful of stores, if it existed at all. A pickpocket might prey on a random customer, once in a while stealing a wallet. A purse snatcher might make off with the occasional purse. A strong-arm robber might force the cashier to empty her till. Whatever mishap occurred, however, would be local and limited. For both merchant and criminal, a non-networked world offers sharply limited opportunity.

Although it had invested handsomely in digital security, Target Corporation came off looking desperately clueless that 2013 holiday season. No offense to Target, but its people were even more in the dark than this step-by-step consideration of the breach suggests. For while Target thought of itself as the victim of a particular criminal attack, it was actually the victim of a global civilization so intensively networked that the most remote lives and destinies, invisible to one another, cross, interact, collide, and embrace every moment of every day. A refrigeration contractor based in Sharpsburg, Pennsylvania, opens an email attachment and infects his computer, which thereby connects the second-largest retailer in America, headquartered in Minneapolis, Minnesota, along with as many as 70 million of its customers, to predatory thieves working out of Odessa, Ukraine, on the other side of the planet. These malefactors may be part of organized crime networks linked to governments in Moscow or Kiev.

The cost to Target, banks, and credit card companies added up to hundreds of millions of dollars. The cost to individual customers? By the time Target issued a press release on December 19, 2013, Kelly Warpechowski, age twenty-three, living in Milwaukee, had already been notified by her bank that "someone in Russia had spent $900 at 'an oil company' using her card." That very night, the Navy Federal Credit Union alerted Jamie Doyle, a sailor from Chesapeake, Virginia, that he was the victim of fraud. He was at sea, deployed on a Navy warship, at the time, but his wife, Tracy, went shopping the next morning only to discover that her debit card had been drained. "We were literally going in to buy our Christmas dinner, and we had no money." Neither Target, nor Kelly, nor Jamie, nor Tracy saw the connections. How could they have?[28]

Yet we all need at the very least to recognize that the connections exist. In his 2016 book *The Seventh Sense: Power, Fortune, and Survival in the Age of Networks,* consultant and author Joshua Cooper Ramo writes of how "linking our bodies, our cities, our ideas—everything, really—together introduces a genuinely new dynamic to our world. It creates hyperdense concentrations of power. It breeds fresh chances for complex and instant chaos. To follow the logic of the French philosopher Paul Virilio for a moment, 'When you invent the ship, you also invent the shipwreck. When you invent the plane, you also invent the plane crash.' Surely we can count on the network to invent the network accident—and many of them." Ramo observes that the "pre-network instinct to *fear Chinese!* or *Fear Spanish!* is the wrong one. . . . *Fear deflation? Fear ISIS? Fear the RMB [Chinese Yuan]?* Such fear reflects a blindness. Finance, terrorism, and currency change when they are connected. It's the network we should be nervous about."[29]

Yes! Target *should* have been "nervous about" their network. Yet when they were warned, not once but twice, that intruders were in their house, they did nothing. If an intruder had walked in the front door of a Target store, strolled through a checkout lane, and held up a POS, they would at least have called the cops. Why did they ignore alarms that detected a cyberintruder? According to cybersecurity experts *The Daily Mail* interviewed in 2014, Target is routinely "bombarded with alerts. They get so many that they just don't respond to everything." In fact, as *The Daily Mail* pointed out, the FireEye software Target used "has a function that automatically deletes malicious software, but it had been turned off by Target's security team before the hackers' attack." This is what "the vast majority" of FireEye's users do because there are so many false positives. An "automated" security system requires "love and care and feeding," according to the experts the British newspaper talked to. "You have to watch it and monitor it."[30]

WATCH AND MONITOR: ARE WE HUMAN BEINGS UP TO THE TASK?

In *Resilience: Why Things Bounce Back,* Andrew Zolli and Ann Marie Healy write of the "incomprehensible complexity, interconnectivity, and volatility of the modern world—one in which upheavals can appear to be triggered by seemingly harmless events, arrive with little warning, and reveal hidden, almost absurd correlations in their wake." As for the "contributions of the much-ballyhooed Information Age, just having more data doesn't automatically help." Too many alerts are just as bad as too few. Maybe worse, the IT experts told *The Daily Mail.* "After all," Zolli and Healy continue, "if we could actually see each of the individual packets of data pulsing through the Internet . . . could we make sense of them?"[31]

The answer—which is *no*—underscores an ineluctable fact of life in our intensively interconnected environment. When digital networks work well, the result is extraordinary—a nearly frictionless interchange of data, ideas, commerce, and increasingly, control and command of real-world devices that are nodes on the Internet of Things. But when something goes wrong, the result may or may not be catastrophic, but it is quite often both crippling and bewildering. This is true even when the problem is a technical glitch rather than a premeditated attack. In separate incidents, "computer problems" forced Southwest Airlines (July 2016) and

Delta Airlines (August 8, 2016) to cancel flights and ground perfectly good aircraft operated and maintained by perfectly able employees. On July 8 of the year before, glitches in routine router upgrades halted trading on the New York Stock Exchange for nearly four hours, forced United Airlines to ground flights, and crashed the servers for WSJ.com.[32] And it is also true when bad actors set out to do nefarious things along the network.

The Target breach was, of course, just one of several cyberattacks with impact sufficient to make international headlines. After the Sony Pictures Entertainment breach of November 2014, in which a hacker outfit announcing itself as the Guardians of Peace (GOP) leaked internal emails and PII of company executives and employees—everything from embarrassing gossip and personal sniping to Social Security numbers—U.S. officials accused the North Korean government of launching the attack in retaliation for Sony's release of the anti-Kim Jong-un satiric comedy *The Interview* (although a significant number of digital security and forensics experts disagreed with this attribution).[33] Sony responded by pulling the national release of the film, but allowed a handful of independent exhibitors to show the movie at their own risk. For his part, President Barack Obama criticized Sony's decision, remarking in a December 19, 2014 press conference, "We cannot have a society in which some dictator someplace can start imposing censorship here in the United States."[34] But this sentence from the president's press conference expresses *precisely* the lesson of the Sony breach. Global digital interconnectivity *has* created such a society. Someone someplace *can* impose a variety of actions on somebody else somewhere else. Just consider those Russian cyberattacks on the DNC and WikiLeaks' decision to release the stolen data on July 22, 2016, the weekend before the Democratic National Convention.[35]

The Target, Sony, and DNC breaches have at least three things in common.

First: All were network attacks. The common term "cyberattack" is misleading because the even more common term "cyberspace" is a figure of speech that has outlived its usefulness. So-called cyber*space* is not "space" at all. It is a global network of interconnected local networks and the devices on them. It is a physical, real-world complex.

Second: The attacks all had remote—*extremely* remote—origins. To paraphrase President Obama's description of North Korea's presumed role in the Sony breach, all were instances of somebody someplace imposing something on institutions and individuals somewhere else, which, in all three cases, happened to be the United States. Indeed, all the attacks may—*may*—have been in some measure sanctioned by foreign governments.

Third: All these attacks in so-called *cyber*space had serious consequences in so-called *real*space. Entities, companies, enterprises, governments, nations, and individuals were victimized by entities, companies, enterprises, governments, and individuals remote from them, with whom they had no formal, familial, political, or business relationship. Thanks to digital networks, isolation was no obstacle to—or defense against—the attacks and their consequences.

Unfair? You bet.

Unfathomable? Pretty much.

A fact of life today? The *essence* of life today.

RESILIENCE: THE BETTER BOAT WE MUST LEARN TO BUILD

The Identity Theft Research Center reported having identified a total of 584 breaches in the United States during the first seven months of 2016. These exposed a total of 20,525,697 records.[36] *SecurityWeek* reported the online theft (by "hacking") of 121,199,741 records worldwide in 2015, up from 67,057,537 in 2014 and 48,805,381 in 2013. Compare this to theft of records by "physical loss"—1,100 records reported worldwide in 2015, down from 20,358 in 2014 and 24,533 in 2013. Data thieves have all but stopped carrying off bundles of paper.[37] In 2016, the Ponemon Institute surveyed 383 companies in 12 countries and discovered that the average total cost of a data breach is $4 million. Per stolen record, this amounts to an average cost of $158.[38]

ACTION ITEM

You are not alone. Attacks and outright breaches are plentiful. Understandably, you may be reluctant to report an incident that affects your organization. The Department of Homeland Security urges all companies to report cyber incidents as a means of enhancing the security and resilience of the business community. See https://www.dhs.gov/how-do-i/report-cyber-incidents. There is ample precedent for reporting other business problems, including 800 numbers for anonymous whistleblower reporting of bad actors within a corporation. The C-suite and the board must develop an unambiguous policy on reporting cyber incidents.

"If we cannot control the volatile tides of change," the authors of *Resilience* write, "we can learn to build better boats. We can design—and redesign—organizations, institutions, and systems to better absorb disruption, operate under a wider variety of conditions, and shift more fluidly from one circumstance to the next."[39]

Indeed, for years now, engineers, scientists, and policymakers, among others, have been looking at the world and have been asking, "What causes one system to break and another to rebound? How much change can a system absorb and still retain its integrity and purpose? What characteristics make a system adaptive to change?" Most important, they have asked, "In an age of constant disruption, how do we build in better shock absorbers for ourselves, our communities, companies, economies, societies, and the planet?"[40] Now those who create and manage digital networks and the nodes strung along them must ask and answer these same questions with the object of building better shock absorbers.

Still, as a concept and a value, resilience is not new even to digital systems. The Internet is an American invention, beginning in 1969 as ARPANET with funds from the Department of Defense's Advanced Research Projects Agency (ARPA, predecessor of DARPA). ARPANET was commissioned by the military to make its defense-related C^3 (Command, Control, and Communications) systems more resilient. Defense planners were worried that if an enemy managed to knock out telephone and other conventional communications system, the American military would be effectively decapitated. A network of computers, however, could still function and thus maintain C^3. National security expert Richard A. Clarke has observed that, despite its military pedigree, the Internet was the work of liberal scientists and engineers—hippies, really—who "did not want [the Internet] to be controlled by governments, either singly or collectively, and so they designed a system that placed a higher priority on decentralization than on security."[41] Actually, this decentralization turned out to be one of the sources of the Internet's security through resilience. Robert Kahn, among the small group of computer scientists broadly credited with having "invented" the Internet, laid down from the get-go four principles that remain basic to the Internet today:

1. Each network on the Internet must stand on its own and should require no internal changes to connect to the Internet.
2. Communication should be technically forgiving. If a data packet fails to make it to its final destination, it should be rapidly and automatically retransmitted from its source.
3. "Gateways" and "routers" (these terms came later than the concepts behind them) interconnect the networks of the Internet. Their function is to pass data packets; therefore, they should retain no information about the individual packets.
4. There is no global control of the Internet at the operations level. It is a decentralized network.[42]

Yet it is also true that the essential openness at the heart of the Internet, a structure that welcomes rather than shuns connection, creates its own vulnerabilities. These are potential targets the builders and users of analog communications systems—pre-digital telephone networks and simple radio broadcasting—could not have begun to envision. So, we are left with the question: "If our connections to the world are the sources of both our power and our vulnerability, how do we achieve true digital resilience?"

Answering this question demands that we learn more in six areas, which are the subjects of the chapters that follow:

- Resilient and nonresilient systems in our world
- The theory of networks

- The digital networks to which we are connected
- How our digital networks can be visualized, modeled, and dynamically monitored
- How the resilience—and nonresilience—of our networks can be measured and scored, so that vulnerabilities can be surfaced and prioritized for modification and remediation
- Formulating a resilient response

Nothing we do can purge the many threats from our intensively networked digital environment. Our only choice, then, is to accept our universe of risk and to inform ourselves more fully and purposefully about it, so that we can design into our digital systems the resilience they require not merely to allow us to survive in digital reality, but to thrive in it. This is not as hard as it sounds, but it does take commitment and leadership. And the leadership to implement a digitally resilient standard in one's network starts in the C-suite, with the CEO.

TAKEAWAY

Today's intensively interactive digitally networked environment creates unprecedented opportunity and vulnerability for businesses. Digital security is mandatory, but insufficient, to prevent cyberattacks. In time, every business connected to the Internet—indeed, every Internet user—will be attacked. The only rational choice is to accept the risks that accompany opportunity and design resilience into our digital systems and our business policies, structures, and operations. The organizations that survive and thrive today and tomorrow are and will be resilient.

2

HARD TO BREAK

Resilience—A Winning Strategy in a Losing War

Seventy-six percent of respondents to the 2016 *Cyberthreat Defense Report* from CyberEdge Group reported having been compromised by a successful cyberattack within the previous twelve months. This was up from 71 percent in 2015 and 62 percent in 2014. Moreover, 62 percent of respondents reported believing that they would suffer a successful cyberattack in the coming year (up from 52 percent in 2015 and 38 percent in 2014).[1] The average consolidated total cost of a data breach in 2016 was $4 million, up from $3.8 million the year before.[2] No wonder one digital security firm recently described its industry as continuing "to fight a losing war against cyberattackers" and doing so "even as data breaches and security compromises have become unfortunate realities of transacting in today's digitized economies."[3] Even Kaspersky Lab, a maker of popular antivirus and security programs, disclosed on its blog the discovery of "an advanced attack" on its own internal networks. Kaspersky called the exploit Duqu 2.0, a malware program that acts "as a backdoor into the system and facilitates the theft of private information."[4]

I invite you to unpack the information you just read. First: More than three-quarters of organizations surveyed reported having been exploited by at least one successful cyberattack in a year. Second: On average, successful cyberattacks are very costly. Third: A major cybersecurity firm describes the war that it and its colleagues and competitors are prosecuting as "a losing war." Fourth: The "losing war" poses an existential threat to everyone "transacting in today's digitized economies" precisely because everyone does business in these economies. Fifth: Even an extraordinarily high level of sophistication in matters of digital security will not save your enterprise from attack; Kaspersky is an established cybersecurity firm. "From a threat actor point of view," Kaspersky Lab's Global Research & Analysis Team (GReAT) wrote, "the decision to target a world-class security company must be quite difficult." This decision suggests that the attackers are "either . . . very confident they won't get caught, or perhaps they don't care much if they are discovered and exposed."[5] So, sixth: Everyone is vulnerable, especially since (at least some) highly skilled attackers are willing to go for broke in attacking the hardest of hard targets.

Kaspersky hasn't found the silver bullet of cybersecurity because cybersecurity will never be sufficient. That is why digital resilience is necessary. Of course, digital resilience is no silver bullet, either. It will not resolve all vulnerabilities. It will not eliminate all faults. It will allow you to survive an attack, identify a breach, and contain it as quickly as possible—while, in the meantime, continuing to remain connected and doing business.

FIGHTING A LOSING WAR: WE ALREADY KNOW HOW

Intensively networked business—a brave new world? More like a grave new world. Except that there is really nothing new about it. To live is to fight a losing war—not 76 percent of the time, but 100 percent of the time. Hard-edged Darwinism turns out not to be a case of survival of the fittest, but survival of the most resilient. The people, organisms, organizations, nations, machines, and systems that most thoroughly achieve resilience survive not only the longest but also the most productively. Being alive, at work, and out and about in the world means that you *will* suffer attack. Perhaps it will come in the form of a mugger in a dark alley, an unwelcome letter from the IRS in your mailbox, an infection by an antibiotic-resistant strain of microbe in your lung, or a really wicked hangover. Whatever form the attack may take, nobody escapes forever. You can't be strong enough, smart enough, or fast enough to evade every assault. Resilience is real. The resilient have the best chance not only of survival but of prospering after—even under—an attack.

This has always been the case. And as Rockefeller Foundation president Judith Rodin observed in her 2014 *The Resilience Dividend: Being Strong in a World Where Things Go Wrong,* it has never been more urgently the case than it is today:

> In the twenty-first century, building resilience is one of our most urgent social and economic issues because we live in a world that is defined by disruption. Not a month goes by that we don't see some kind of disturbance to the normal flow of life somewhere: a cyber-attack, a new strain of virus, a structural failure, a violent storm, a civil disturbance, an economic blow, a natural system threatened.[6]

Disruption, Rodin observes, is something "the world has always known . . . but there are three disruptive phenomena that are distinctly modern: urbanization, climate change, and globalization."[7] The first and third of these have a critically important digital dimension, namely the pervasive connectivity of the digital network, which is both a *driver* of contemporary civilization and a *threat* to it. The point is that resilience is not a "bonus feature" of, or an "optional accessory" to, every productive activity and enterprise in the twenty-first century. It must be at their core, a necessity to them. Resilience has always been important, just never more urgently indispensable. Moreover, today's intensive and ubiquitous connectivity has made resilience the table stakes for any enterprise interested in survival. If you want more than survival, you need to think of resilience as both a baseline requirement *and* a means of gaining competitive advantage.

HOW MUCH RESILIENCE IS ENOUGH RESILIENCE?

Let's start at the baseline. Let's say your expectations are modest. Let's say you run a business that is only minimally connected, at least by comparison, say, with a 100 percent online merchant like Amazon. How much resilience do *you* really need, even in today's world?

Dyn is an Internet performance management company. Among other things, Dyn products control much of the Internet's domain name system (DNS) infrastructure. The DNS has been a feature of the Internet since its invention and is at the very core of Internet functionality. IP addresses are as necessary to locating and identifying services and devices on the Internet as street addresses are necessary to locating and identifying homes and businesses and people in a city, town, village, or country lane. The DNS translates human-understandable names of places on the Internet into numerical IP addresses such as 199.181.131.249. If these numbers mean something to you, congratulations, you are a prodigious Internet geek with too much time on your hands. For everyone else, however, they form a meaningless sequence of numbers. Thanks to DNS, however, Disney.com becomes 199.181.131.249, and your browser goes there.

"On Friday October 21, 2016 from approximately 11:10 UTC to 13:20 UTC and then again from 15:50 UTC until 17:00 UTC, Dyn came under attack by two large and complex Distributed Denial of Service (DDoS) attacks against our Managed DNS infrastructure." The good news, as reported by Dyn's own analysis, is that the "attacks were successfully mitigated by Dyn's Engineering and Operations teams." The bad news: "but not before significant impact was felt by our customers and their end users."[8] Those customers included websites belonging to "Twitter, the Guardian, Netflix, Reddit, CNN, and many others in Europe and the U.S.," according to *The Guardian*, making the attack the largest of its kind—ever.[9]

Now, in addition to good news and bad news, *The Guardian* also pointed to what it called some "interesting" news. Distributed denial of service is a common type of attack, which, typically, is not particularly sophisticated. The objective of a DDoS exploit is to bombard the servers of a targeted network with so many requests that the network collapses under the strain, becoming impossible to contact. Because it is usually impractical for an attacker to organize enough confederates to launch a coordinated attack, DDoS exploits are usually mounted by infecting as many computers as possible with a type of malware that transforms each infected computer into a bot, as in ro*bot*. The bot can be made to do things like send repeated requests to a targeted system. The bot can also propagate itself, infecting other computers, thereby creating a botnet, a network of coordinated bots, which collectively bombard a targeted system with connection requests. A large botnet can quickly overwhelm and disable even websites built to handle huge volumes of traffic.

But this is not the "interesting" part of what happened on October 21, 2016. In fact, it is routine. No, what makes the attack on Dyn "interesting is that [it] was orchestrated using a weapon called the Mirai botnet. Unlike other botnets, which are typically made up of computers, the Mirai botnet is largely made up of so-called "Internet of Things" (IoT) devices such as digital cameras and DVR players."[10] Actually *The Guardian* is being very modest in citing just two examples of nodes on the IoT. The variety is much, much greater—and growing. "For many years, the only important computing device in a typical home or business was the personal computer (PC), first on the desktop and then on the laptop," the authors of *Trillions: Thriving in the Emerging Information Technology* write. They point out that in "the past few years," these computing form factors have been eclipsed by smartphones and tablets. They go on to use the phrase "pervasive computing," which they define in reference "to the assumption . . . that this transition" from desktop to smartphone, "dramatic though it is, is just the first step in a far more fundamental change. Rather than moving computation out of one kind of box into other—smaller and more portable—boxes, by the end of this transition computing will for all practical purposes be confined to no box at all. Computation (and thus data) will all but literally have escaped into the ambient environment."[11]

Pause here for two observations. First, the "all but literally" is an important modification of "have escaped." The fact is that computing devices are indeed escaping *confinement to boxes,* but they are not escaping *connection to the Internet.* They are connected. Second, much of the "transition" the *Trillions* authors describe is well under way—and has made tremendous progress since 2012, when the book was published. Even back then, the authors conceded that we "already put microprocessors into nearly every significant thing that we manufacture, and we are quickly figuring out how to make those processors usefully communicate with each other, and with us. . . . We are . . . well on our way to a world with trillions of computers."[12]

What will these trillions of unboxed, ambient computers add up to? They "will quickly coalesce into something new and disruptive: an *environment* of computation. Not computation that we *use,* but computation that we *live* in . . . houses [that] cater to our whims; power grids [that] become intelligent; and tractors [that] drive themselves through fields sown not just with seeds, but also with millions of 'smart dust' moisture and nutrient sensors."[13] We are moving toward this computation environment rapidly. For instance, right now, in 2016, the "average car . . . can have between 25 and 50 central processing units (CPUs)," which are, in fact, unboxed computers. Many, not all, of these automotive CPUs are networked.[14]

So, back to that Mirai botnet *The Guardian* found so "interesting." The Internet of Things is much bigger—has many more nodes—than the Internet that is populated with desktops, laptops, smartphones, and tablets. "Because it has so many internet-connected devices to choose from, attacks from Mirai are much larger than what most DDoS attacks could previously achieve. Dyn estimated that the attack had involved '100,000 malicious endpoints,' and the company . . . said there had been reports of an extraordinary attack strength of 1.2Tbps"—1.2 trillion bytes per second! "One trillion . . . bytes per second," according to the online *PC Magazine Encyclopedia,* "is a measurement that prior to the twenty-first century was unthinkable."[15] In terms of a volume of data, consider that 1,428 CD-ROMS are required to store 1 terabyte. So, Dyn servers had the equivalent of 1,428 CD-ROMS thrown at them every second during the attack. If the reports are true and accurate, they reveal an attack that was "roughly twice as powerful as any similar attack on record." The evidence points to the October 2016 attack, massive as it was, as having been mounted by a non-state group. David Fidler, adjunct senior fellow for cybersecurity at the Council on Foreign Relations, asks us to "imagine what a well-resourced state actor could do with insecure IoT devices."[16]

Before the advent of the computer, let alone the networked computer, the world was a hazardous place from which no one escaped some harm before suffering the ultimate harm, namely death. Because evasion of harm is inefficient and, in the long run, impossible, resilience has always been a must—at least for those who wish to survive, let alone thrive. Historically, digital networks have conveyed attacks against mainframes, desktops, and laptops. These digital networks thus added another threat to a physical world that was already threatening even in the pre-digital days. The Internet of Things does not merely heap more digital threats on top of the physical world. Because the IoT is *part* of the physical world, the threats it harbors are not compartmentalized in a strictly digital realm. They are threats in the world. Period. An unboxed "*computation* environment" is part of "*the* environment."

How much resilience is enough for the most modestly connected of enterprises? The answer is about as much as the most intensively connected. In a digital environment of trillions of connections, we are all far more thoroughly networked than we know.

DIGITAL RESILIENCE IS RESILIENCE. PERIOD.

Thanks to the trillions of interconnected nodes of the rapidly evolving IoT, the concept of resilience can no longer be thought of as a figure of speech, a metaphor borrowed from the analog world of nature and nations. Digital resilience is very rapidly becoming as important as the physical resilience of organisms, people, corporations, commercial aircraft, governments, and ecosystems because the IoT is evolving into a bionic system thoroughly embedded in our world and lives. We don't need technologists and tech journalists to tell us this. We all feel it. Back in the 1980s, the most complex piece of electronics most ordinary consumers had to deal with was a VCR. The result was that we became a planet of VCRs perpetually flashing *12:00* because many human beings could not, or stubbornly refused to, master the simple task of setting the digital clock on their machines. Today, we have all been pressed into service as our own personal "IT departments," exercising considerable technical expertise to set up our new smartphones, deal with a plethora of passwords and PINs, figure out whether to answer the ads pleading with us to switch from copper to fiber, sort out why our Internet connection is so slow, even install our own routers and RAM.

Some of us enjoy getting under the hood with our technology. But some of us resent having to make so many banal technical choices. Nevertheless, as Joshua Cooper Ramo writes in *The Seventh Sense: Power, Fortune, and Survival in the Age of Networks,* "Banal technical choices will reverberate through our future with the same influence that the Bill of Rights, the Magna Carta, the Analects of Confucius, and the Koran retain long after they were first written down." Why? Because "many of the technical choices we're about to make will be strikingly political." They will determine who "has access to what data" or where the line is drawn between "human choice and machine intelligence."[17]

This sounds hyperbolic. But give it a chance. "The real contests ahead will concern networks," Ramo writes, "but this means, in fact, a deeper conflict over values." Why? Because networks are not just silicon, wire, and fiber. They "are like churches or schools or congresses; they reflect the aims and ethics of the people who build them." They are contiguous and intertwined extensions of human and social and economic values. Ramo quotes the French philosopher Bruno Latour, who writes that modern societies "cannot be described without recognizing them as having a fibrous, threadlike, wiry, stringy, ropy, capillary character that is never captured by the notions of levels, layers, territories, spheres, categories structure, systems." We are already well aware that (as Ramo summarizes) "borders, like the ones dividing science and politics or military power and civilian safety, begin to erode when everything is linked. Computing machines and networks were once locked into usefully narrow silos, unconnected: An ATM. A heart monitor. A power grid. But now they overlap and inform one another."[18]

Here Ramo is describing the rapid evolution of the IoT, yet the phenomenon underlying that digital evolution is not exclusively the product of digital networks. True, the explosive new direction of digital networks, the growth from millions to billions to trillions of interconnected nodes on a global network, accelerates the destruction of borders and the replacement of levels, layers, and the rest with networks.

But relationships, specifically networks of relationships, have always shaped the real world. Ramo cites Conway's Law, a principle articulated by a computer programmer named Melvin Conway in 1967 (and given its status as "law" by others, the following year): "Organizations which design systems . . . are constrained to produce designs which are copies of the communication structures of these organizations."[19] Conway noted that designing software required collaboration among the authors of that software and that, therefore, the software interfaces that structure a system reflect the social boundaries, the social networks, the social structures, of the organization or organizations whose personnel produced the software. As such, Conway's Law is the inverse of what we have just been talking about. Yes, digital networks (structures with software at their core) shape the "real" (non-digital) world; however, the social aspects of that real, physical world shape software design and, ultimately, digital networks. Put another way: If virtual reality shapes and reshapes the physical world, the physical world shapes and reshapes virtual reality. The relationship between digital networks and the non-digital networks that make up the physical world—and that existed long before computers and computer networks—is truly and intensively interactive and intertwined. This being the case, where resilience is concerned, digital networks should be at least as resilient as the non-digital networks they connect with, amplify, and extend.

DIGITAL RESILIENCE: LEARNING FROM THE ANALOG WORLD

I hold this truth to be self-evident, that the resilience of digital networks should model the resilience of the most resilient organisms, ecosystems, organizations, infrastructures, nations, and people that we know. Back in 1974, Jimmy Treybig founded Tandem Computers, Inc., a company that designed and produced "fault-tolerant" computers for what was then the emerging technology of online transaction processing (OLTP) systems for ATM networks and other banking applications, stock exchanges, commercial transaction processing, and so on. Advertising their products as "NonStop Systems," Tandem incorporated a high-speed "failover" approach to computer design, using multiple processors, redundant storage devices and controllers, and backup power systems. The machines were built not in a fruitless effort to avoid or prevent failure, but to be fault-tolerant—that is, to be sufficiently resilient to operate in cases of inevitable failure, whether caused accidentally or nefariously.[20] This was the 1970s and 1980s, and, as I will point out in Chapter 4, even the early Internet incorporated key aspects of resilient design. Nevertheless, deep into the second decade of the twenty-first century, we have yet to apply to our digital networks anything approaching the level of resilience we have long applied to everything from folding ladders to advanced aircraft—and even to at least some computer systems. We need to get at least as serious about digital resilience as we have been about resilience in other, non-digital systems.

ACTION ITEM

Guaranteed: There are vulnerabilities—faults—in your network. We know this, because there are vulnerabilities in every network. We also know this because humans are involved. And human error is inevitable. We're not perfect. We also can guarantee that, over time, a hacker will find and exploit the vulnerabilities. The most effective strategy to prevent an attacker from bringing down your network is to design resilience into your systems. Resilience will not strengthen all weak points. It will not eliminate all faults. It will, however, create a network that is fault-tolerant. It will allow you to survive an attack, identify a breach, and contain it—while, in the meantime, continuing to remain connected and doing business.

Now, precisely because the relationship between our digital and non-digital networks is interactive—runs two ways—we must acknowledge that the resilience approach can be especially challenging. Even before digital networks became globally pervasive, changes in network design could still create profound changes in "real-life economic patterns." As an instance of this, Ramo cites the expansion of airline routes to Indonesia in the early 1980s, such as those from Hong Kong to Bali, which "brought manufacturing, investment, tipsy expatriates, and then surfers." He goes on to predict that, in our connected age, "the design of research studies, voter databases, genetic-information sharing networks, financial webs . . . will change many usual patterns even as they establish some completely new ones." Ramo quotes investor Paul Graham: "When you decide what infrastructure to use for a project, you're not just making a technical decision. You're also making a social decision, and this may be the more important of the two."

Yet at least equally important are the effects that lie outside of the designers' vision and contemplation. Ramo notes that "networks will be used in ways their designers never imagined—Twitter turned to terror recruitment, Bitcoin as an alternative to central banks."[21] Digital networks can, may, and do reshape the physical world in ways that are not only unintended, unforeseen, and perhaps even unwanted, but they can do this in ways that challenge both the resilience of digital networks and the resilience of aspects of the physical world. A digital network, the Internet, becomes an enabler of the popular and political networks that wrought positive, democratic transformations of the Arab Spring (the Tunisian Revolution was branded the "Twitter Revolution") as well as the terrorist networks that have spawned and nurtured ISIS.

Or, as we saw in Chapter 1, the very digital network that was instrumental in the success of retail giant Target threatened that success by serving as a royal road to attack Target and its customers. The twelve months that followed the December 2013 attack "were tumultuous for the retailer and many of its peers," and the attack proved to be "just the beginning of a series of massive retail data assaults that would expose critical weaknesses in enterprise data security and payment systems." Nevertheless, a ZDNet article published at the end of November 2015 observes, "Target has largely recovered from the breach in terms both of consumer trust and financial impact."[22] The recovery is a testament to the resilience of Target as well as the resilience of its customers and modern consumers in general. The question remains, will retailers and others be motivated to emulate and embody this instance of physical-world resilience in the design, operation, and maintenance of their digital networks?

"The concept of resilience is a powerful lens through which we can view major issues afresh," the authors of *Resilience: Why Things Bounce Back* tell us. They cite everything "from business planning (how do we hedge our corporate strategy to deal with unforeseen circumstances?) to social development (how do we improve the resilience of a community at risk?) to urban planning (how do we ensure the continuity of urban services in the face of a disaster?) to national energy security (how do we achieve the right mix of energy sources and infrastructure to contend with inevitable shocks to the system?)."[23] Since we live in a world in which digital and non-digital networks interconnect, in which virtual reality and physical reality exist in an interactive relationship with one another, studying resilience in the physical world can be helpful in improving the resilience in our digital networks.

Indeed, innovative thinkers such as Joshua Cooper Ramo treat networks as structures that transcend the categories, compartments, or silos in which we traditionally put fields of inquiry and endeavor.

Looking at the examples in the preceding paragraph, Ramo would certainly argue that the relevant discussions are not about business planning, social development, urban planning, and national energy security. In fact, there should be no *discussions*—only a single *discussion* about the single relevant topic, namely networks.

In February 2008, the journal *Nature* published a "News & Views" item titled "Ecology for Bankers," which discussed a "high-level conference" sponsored two years earlier by two apparently disparate organizations, the U.S. National Academies/National Research Council and the Federal Reserve Bank of New York. The objective of this out-of-the-box, almost random-seeming collaboration was to "stimulate fresh thinking on systemic risk" by "bringing together experts from various backgrounds to explore parallels between systemic risk in the financial sector and in selected domains in engineering, ecology, and other fields of science." In other words, these experts in apparently unrelated fields gathered to discuss the one relevant topic they shared: networks. They held in common the thesis that "catastrophic changes in the overall state of a system can ultimately derive from how it is organized"—how it is interconnected, or networked, including "feedback mechanisms within [the network], and from linkages that are latent and often unrecognized." A catastrophic change in a system "may be initiated by some obvious external event, such as a war, but is more usually triggered by a seemingly minor happenstance or even an unsubstantial rumor. Once set in motion, however, such changes can become explosive and afterward will typically exhibit some form of hysteresis, such that recovery is much slower than the collapse. In extreme cases, the changes may be irreversible."[24] (In this case, "hysteresis" takes the form of echoes or repetitions of the original trigger event. A financial panic, for instance, tends to feed off of itself, long after the trigger event has ended.)

The potential for such catastrophic network failures "is widely applicable: for global climate change, as the greenhouse blanket thickens; for 'ecosystem services,' as species are removed; for fisheries, as stocks are overexploited; and for electrical grids or the Internet, as increasing demands are placed on both." For anyone who runs a business, among the most pertinent questions raised by this exuberantly interdisciplinary conference concern risk-management priorities: "First, how much money is spent on studying systemic risk as compared with that spent on conventional risk management in individual firms? Second, how expensive is a systemic-risk event to a national or global economy (examples being the stock market crash of 1987, or the turmoil of 1998 associated with the Russian loan default, and the subsequent collapse of the hedge fund Long-Term Capital Management)? The answer to the first question is 'comparatively very little'; to the second, 'hugely expensive.'"[25]

These questions remain just as pertinent but even more interesting when we learn that an "analogous situation exists within fisheries management," a field apparently remote from the concerns of most businesspeople:

> For the past half-century, investments in fisheries science have focused on management on a species-by-species basis (analogous to single-firm risk analysis). Especially with collapses of some major fisheries, however, this approach is giving way to the view that such models may be fundamentally incomplete, and that the wider ecosystem and environmental context (by analogy, the full banking and market system) are required for informed decisionmaking.[26]

So "to what extent can study of ecosystems inform the design of financial networks in, for instance, their robustness against perturbation?" The conference experts concluded: "Identifying structural attributes shared by these diverse systems that have survived rare systemic events, or have indeed been shaped by them, could provide clues about which characteristics of complex systems correlate with a high degree of robustness."[27]

DIGITAL RESILIENCE: BORROWING KEY CHARACTERISTICS FROM THE PHYSICAL WORLD

While "robustness" is not a synonym for *resilience,* it comes close, and the conference experts pointed to "work on the network structure of communities of pollinators and the plants they pollinate." Those who studied these biological communities described them as "networks [that] are disassortative," a term that describes a network in which "highly connected 'large' nodes tend to have their connections disproportionately with 'small' nodes; conversely, small nodes connect with disproportionately few large ones." From this observation, the experts concluded that "disassortative networks tend to confer a significant degree of stability against disturbance." That is, the quality of being disassortive—disproportionately connecting big nodes to many small nodes and small nodes to few big ones—enhances the resilience of a network. Additionally, "ecologists and others have long suggested that modularity—the degree to which the nodes of a system can be decoupled into relatively discrete components—can promote robustness." This observation prompted some conference experts to point out that "a basic principle in the management of forest fires and epidemics is that if there is strong interconnection among all elements, a perturbation will encounter nothing to stop it from spreading. But once the system is appropriately compartmentalized—by firebreaks, or vaccination of 'superspreaders'—disturbance or risk is more easily countered."[28]

Digital network architects should find abundant food for thought in this discussion of network architecture across multiple fields. The conference participants warned, however, that neither disassortativeness nor modularity were the silver bullets of robustness or resilience because "modularity will often involve a trade-off between local and systemic risk." With regard specifically to financial markets, "the wrong compartmentalization . . . could preclude stabilizing feedbacks, such as mechanisms for maintaining liquidity of cash flows through the financial system, where fragmentation leading to illiquidity could actually increase systemic risk (as in the bank runs leading to the Great Depression)." The larger point, however, is that there is much to be learned about creating resilient networks from the "topology of financial networks," specifically the "interplay between network topology and random or targeted 'attack,'" which provides "insights for the control of infectious diseases and the defence of networks such as the Internet."[29]

The authors of *Resilience* argue that many resilient systems are diverse at their edges but simple at the core, citing "DNA in a cell, or the communications protocols governing the Internet," both of which are "specialized languages [that] encode a vast menagerie of inputs and outputs, yet as protocols, they remain utterly basic, evolving slowly, if at all."[30] Still, it is often difficult to design networks that are resilient both against known or anticipated threats and in the face of unknown, unrecognized, or unanticipated threats. For instance, an arborist might design a tree farm with roads strategically placed as fire breaks in anticipation of the well-known threat of forest fires, yet those same roads make possible the unintentional importation of an invasive beetle, an entirely unanticipated hazard that may end up destroying all the trees on the farm. The problem with designing for resilience is the possibility of creating so-called robust-yet-fragile (RYF) systems. The RYF problem typifies the trade-offs designers of networks may have to make "between efficiency and fragility on the one hand and inefficiency and robustness on the other." The most efficient tree farm would be very densely planted. Yet such a tree farm would also be the most vulnerable to the known hazard of a calamitous forest fire. Plant your tree farm sparsely to include numerous fire breaks, and you increase resilience, but at the expense of efficiency. A very sparsely planted tree farm is virtually immune to mass damage from forest fires, but it is too inefficient to be profitably productive. The objective is to find a midpoint between the extremes, whether the network in question is physical or digital.[31]

ACTION ITEM

A network can either be secure or efficient. It cannot be both. A secure network has relatively few connections and provides very limited access to data. An efficient network has many connections and provides unrestricted access to data. Avoid the binary either/or trap posed by the goal of "perfect" security by instead embracing maximum resilience, a business strategy that balances security and efficiency on a fulcrum placed between these extremes. Make your network fault-tolerant, and you can risk faults without risking your business.

Beyond this, the most resilient networks are those that possess the ability to reconfigure themselves to adapt to changing circumstances and, when subjected to truly overwhelming stress or attack, "fail gracefully," employing "strategies for avoiding dangerous circumstances, detecting intrusions, minimizing and isolating component damage, diversifying the resources they consume, operating in a reduced state if necessary, and self-organizing to heal in the wake of a breach." The objective in designing resilience is not to achieve perfection. "A seemingly perfect system is often the most fragile, while a dynamic system, subject to occasional failure, can be the most robust. Resilience is, like life itself, messy, imperfect, and inefficient. But it survives."[32]

The most optimistic current statistics predict that at least 76 percent of organizations will suffer a cyberattack in a given year. Over several years, this makes cyberattacks inevitable for virtually every organization. But, as the authors of *Resilience* counsel, this is not a reason to despair. Instead, it should prompt engaging in an effort that complements mitigation. Whatever the network in question, whether physical, social, institutional, or digital, we need to innovate in ways that enable us all to "be prepared and cope with surprises and disruptions, even as we work to fend them off."[33] Resilient networks allow us to survive and to continue to operate as we identify and contain a threat or breach. At the same time, we can also learn from the event, so that we may take steps to defeat or diminish the effect of future attacks. Our networks will never be unbreakable, but they can be made very hard to break.

TAKEAWAY

The risk that your network will be attacked depends, first and foremost, on its size (number of connected users, or "nodes"). The bigger the network, the greater the risk. Given sufficient time, a network of almost any size will be attacked. For this reason, the fight for cybersecurity is a *battle* that cannot be won; however, creating digital resilience keeps you in the fight, so that you need never lose the *war*. While digital resilience is relatively new—because digital technology is relatively new—

the concept of resilience is as old as the evolution of life on this planet. To build resilience into your digital networks is to draw on principles found throughout physical, natural, and human systems from businesses to nations to civilizations. Moreover, because today's Internet encompasses a trillion-plus-node Internet of Things, the line separating digital resilience from the more familiar physical resilience of organisms, people, corporations, commercial aircraft, governments, and ecosystems is rapidly dissolving. Resilience is therefore an essential value of modern life, and by emulating the ubiquitous model of resilience, you can make digital networks hard to break.

3

THE NATURE OF NETWORKS

Knowledge—The First Step Toward Digital Resilience

"When you invent the ship, you also invent the shipwreck," wrote the French philosopher and cultural theorist Paul Virilio.[1] The power of networks is connectivity. The vulnerability of networks is connectivity. But let's identify our vessel properly. It is not the SS *Internet.* It is something much older, because networks are much older.

ALL NETWORKS ARE SOCIAL

Back in 1758, the celebrated taxonomist Carl Linnaeus, who laid the basis for the modern classification of biological species, coined a Latin term for human beings: *Homo sapiens*—"knowing man." Nicholas A. Christakis and James H. Fowler, authors of *Connected: How Your Friends' Friends' Friends Affect Everything You Feel, Think, and Do,* believe it's time for an update to a term that more accurately reflects the true evolutionary status of modern humanity. Their suggestion is *Homo dictyous.* It translates as "network man," which, they argue, better describes a species that has evolved to care about others through social networks. Christakis and Fowler hold that networks have become so central to human existence that they now constitute "a kind of human superorganism," which vastly expands the range of human capability. "Just as brains can do things no single neuron can do, so can social networks do things no single person can do."[2]

While Christakis and Fowler see the evolution of *Homo dictyous* from *Homo sapiens* as relatively recent on the timeline of human evolution, they certainly do not claim any date as recent, say, as 1967, when the plan for the Internet's ancestor, "ARPANET," was published under the auspices of DARPA, or 1983, when the Internet's foundation protocol suite, TCP/IP, was adopted. No, no. Christakis and Fowler see the emergence of Network Man as something that happened some millennia back. Just when is not certain, but it must have come well before the roughly five thousand years of history we have in recorded form. The impulse to record history had to have some motive, and the most compelling motive is a collective desire to *share* a common past. This desire to share implies the existence of social networks.

Social networks were clearly of tremendous value in our cultural evolution, but, if we take Christakis and Fowler's *Homo dictyous* thesis as more than a figure of speech, we must conclude that networks also played a role in our biological evolution as a species. Indeed, they may have served as the nexus at which biological evolution met social evolution. Whatever the stronger driver, biological need, or social imperative, humankind's most foundational inventions have served explicitly to expand humanity's social networks. For instance, the invention of writing in portable forms, about 3200 BCE in Sumer and (independently) in Egypt, enabled individuals to network with one another, governments to network with their people, and governments and peoples to network with other governments and other peoples.[3] In this manner, the boundaries of social networks challenged time and distance in ways that overcame political and even geographical boundaries. Such transcendence of real-world boundaries is, of course, precisely the innovation frequently credited to the ascendency of the Internet in our own day.

ACTION ITEM

The best way to begin to understand digital networks is to understand the nature of social networks. The technology of networking is new. The motives for networking predate recorded history.

One aspect of network-related technology is a connection to seemingly unrelated technologies. For instance, we don't customarily see the development of various vehicles—from the wheel to spacecraft—as a development in *network* technology; nevertheless, vehicle innovation increased both the distance over which written communication could be conveyed and the speed of its conveyance.[4] This, in turn, enhanced humankind's networks and networking capabilities. The transportation of people and cargoes in any considerable quantity must have attracted the attention of monarchs and their border guards even in the ancient world. Substantial shipments and immigration, readily detected, could be to some degree regulated by central authority. But the transportation of written material was far less obvious. Written records are far more portable than crowds of people or bulk cargoes. Even in the pre-digital world, including the ancient world, the central control of social networks was far from total and often quite difficult.

THE RELATIONSHIP BETWEEN DATA AND NETWORKS

Before the advent of printing (a force to be reckoned with in Asia by the ninth century), hand-copied manuscripts were the only available means of reproducing written works in quantity, and manuscripts remained dominant until the evolution of movable-type printing, beginning about 1040 in China and 1450 in the Europe of Johannes Gutenberg. Because hand-copying was labor-intensive and costly, libraries and scriptoria (where, in medieval Europe, manuscripts were both copied and stored, usually in monasteries) became the chief nodes of the knowledge network. Typically, libraries were the creation of the wealthy and powerful and, also often, were the property of religious authorities or secular officials (high priests, popes, cardinals, as well as kings, queens, and other hereditary heads of state). Both the flow and content of written data were therefore largely controlled by the state and those most deeply invested in the state. Nevertheless, these key network nodes were vulnerable to attack and destruction. The great Library of Alexandria, for instance, was created and maintained under the patronage of Egypt's Ptolemaic pharaohs. Built in the third century BCE, it became, arguably, *the* central node of the ancient world's knowledge network. It was not just the largest ancient library (housing perhaps 400,000 papyrus scrolls at its height), it was also an active, real-time research center to which learned persons could travel to meet with others and discuss ideas.[5]

While the Alexandrian library had the patronage, sanction, and protection of the state, it was vulnerable to all manner of attack. In fact, it is less famous today for having existed than for having been destroyed—even though historians and archaeologists continue to debate just which of four major assaults on the library proved definitively destructive. During the Great Roman Civil War (Caesar's Civil War, 49–45 BCE), it suffered a fire in 48 BCE. The third-century Roman emperor Aurelian's conquest of the Palmyrene Empire in AD 270–275 included the restoration of Egypt to the Roman Empire. In the fight to reclaim Egypt, Aurelian burned the Royal Quarter of Alexandria (the "Brucheion") to the ground. If the great library, housed in this neighborhood, had not been totally destroyed by Caesar in 48 BCE, it was almost certainly razed in this massive blaze. In AD 391, the Coptic Christian pope Theophilus of Alexandria may have destroyed the library as part of his campaign of destruction against temples and other structures in the city associated with "pagans." Finally, if the Library of Alexandria had not been obliterated by these three attacks, it may have been (according to at least four Arabic sources) destroyed by order of 'Amr ibn al-'As, commanding Muslim forces in the Muslim conquest of Egypt in 642.[6]

The destruction of the Library of Alexandria may have been incidental to wars of conquest or may have been the deliberate attempt of one ruling power to disrupt the data network of another and even to obliterate the history of a people in a particular time and place. Wikipedia lists 168 notable instances of mass book and manuscript burnings, beginning with the Destruction of Ebla in 2240 BCE, going through the bibliographical bonfires of Adolf Hitler's Nazi Party in 1933, and ending with the book burnings and destruction of cultural monuments by ISIS during 2014–2015.[7]

Indisputably an attack against a network of ideas was the assault by English king Henry VIII against the monasteries during the somewhat euphemistically named Dissolution of the Monasteries.

In several sweeps during 1536–1541, forces dispatched by the newly self-minted Protestant monarch set out to erase any lingering governing authority of what had been the Roman Catholic state church of England. Officially, the dissolution was a state seizure of Roman Catholic church property, including much valuable real estate, income, and other assets, and the dismissal of those clergy who did not submit to the new religious order in England. Tragically, many of the seizures were accompanied by acts of wanton destruction, especially of the monastic scriptoria, where manuscripts, including priceless illuminated manuscripts, were simply discarded or destroyed. Call it a network hack, with the emphasis on the word *hack* in its root meaning.

ACTION ITEM

One of history's greatest lessons is also one of its least heeded. Part one of the lesson is that data is vulnerable. This is evidenced by its frequent loss or outright destruction. In history's most famous instance of data loss, the destruction of the Library of Alexandria, security was elaborate. The library's contents were housed in a great building, protected by a great emperor, in the heart of a great imperial city. So, part two of the lesson is, throughout history, security measures alone have been inadequate the to protect data. Heed the lessons of history. Install security, but create resilience on the historically proven assumption that security, while necessary, is almost never sufficient to the preservation of data.

The storage of flammable records in flammable buildings made for an inherently nonresilient network. Add to this the unique nature of at least some of the manuscripts—either one-offs or reproduced in very few copies—and the network at given nodes became even more vulnerable, not just to accident, but to the intentional acts of literal hackers. The advent of printing, particularly printing with movable type, added great resilience to the world's pre-electronic data and knowledge networks by introducing redundancy in the form of multiple copies of data. The degree of redundancy—the number of copies—was potentially open-ended, provided that at least one copy of a particular work existed from which to set new type and create a new printed edition. Redundancy in and of itself is neither synonymous with resilience nor a substitute for it. It can, however, be an important component of resilience, which is why savvy businesses and individuals continuously back up their files offsite or in the cloud.

Printing made creating redundancy cheaper and faster than making manuscript copies by hand. In turn, the invention of movable type, which allowed *setting* type using an individual "case" of letters, made printing far less time-consuming, skill-intensive, and labor-intensive than carving entire unique book pages one at a time. Typesetting is also far more fault-tolerant than carving a woodblock. Because of its cost-effectiveness and speed, movable type not only made knowledge networks more resilient, it made them larger, arming more nodes with the same data. It decentralized the data networks, which no longer had to be concentrated in a few great libraries or scriptoria, both vulnerable to regime change, religious reformation, and natural disasters.

By the nineteenth century, two new elements of speed and economy were added to Gutenberg's original innovation. The linotype machine allowed the very rapid composition of type, cast into metal "slugs," each of which (typically) created one line of type. The linotype introduced a significant degree of automation into typesetting.

Following this were innovations in the speed of the presses themselves, which ran on steam or (later) electric power. These turned out copies of inexpensive books and, especially, newspapers, pamphlets, broadsides, official government publications, and publications by those opposed to governments in great quantity. This raised redundancy to the status of semi-ubiquity, multiplying the resilience of information networks even further while expanding and decentralizing those networks. Of course, it was still possible to attack information networks. For example, on May 21, 1856, during the run-up to the American Civil War, pro-slavery hooligans attacked an abolitionist newspaper office in Lawrence, Kansas Territory, during a time in which territorial residents were voting on whether to enter the Union as a slaveholding state or a free state. The pro-slavery raiders smashed the newspaper's printing press and threw its stock of type into the Kansas River.[8]

Knowledge networks based on printed matter may also be vulnerable to the machinations of criminal and civil law, which may be used to enjoin printing press owners and publishers from printing and distributing material some party considers objectionable. In the case of a legal challenge to the operation of a press, resilience may consist of hiring a better lawyer than that of the plaintiff. In the case of the violent sack of Lawrence, abolitionists from other parts of the country came to the aid of the town and new presses were purchased. The availability of such sources of aid constituted the resilience of this particular network.

REAL-TIME TRANSMISSION OF DATA

Samuel F. B. Morse's commercially viable version of the telegraph, patented in 1837, launched the era of the analog electronic network, replacing ink and paper with the electrical/electronic creation and transmission of written (or verbal) data and its transcription back into an ink and paper form on the receiving end of the transmission. Telegraphy enabled virtually instantaneous communication, potentially in real-time. There were delays created by the time it took to manually transcribe the electrical signals (the "dots" and "dashes" of the Morse Code) into more universally readable alphabetic language and numerals, and there was the time consumed in delivering messages from the telegraph office to the addressee. On the other hand, in certain applications, communication was in real-time and interactive, even conversational. For instance, a military commander at the front of a battle could communicate telegraphically with higher headquarters in a rear echelon to report on conditions, ask for instructions, request reinforcements, or respond to orders.

In the American Civil War, telegraph wire was run along the rope that tethered manned observation balloons to the ground. This allowed observers aloft to report in real-time on enemy movements and on the effect of artillery fire on the enemy. Commanders on the ground could adjust their tactics, and artillerists their aim. In a historical study of how President Abraham Lincoln used the telegraph to personally direct some of the major action in the Civil War, author Tom Wheeler calls the sixteenth president "the first national leader to project himself electronically. The command and control by email that the evening news showed being employed in a twenty-first-century war [in Iraq] traces its roots to the nineteenth-century American Civil War." Wheeler argues that the "telegraph changed the nature of national executive leadership and provided Abraham Lincoln with a tool that helped him win the Civil War" by "eliminating distance as a controlling factor in the exchange of information, thus allowing coordination among disparate forces and between the national leadership and those forces."[9] Indeed, Steven Spielberg's 2012 film *Lincoln* includes several scenes of the president "running" the war from a basement telegraph room in the War Department's offices.[10]

In addition to providing speed and varying levels of interactivity, telegraphy increased the resilience of information networks by eliminating the need for vulnerable human couriers. There was no Pony Express rider to be ambushed. Furthermore, the interactivity of telegraphy made networks more resilient because errors (garbled messages, ambiguous messages, misunderstood messages, messages with typographical errors) could be readily corrected. The receiving operator or the end recipient could very quickly request clarification, confirmation, retransmission, or correction of doubtful messages—sometimes doing so immediately and interactively.

Within years of its invention, the telegraph expanded into a vast network that one writer on the history of technology dubbed "the Victorian Internet."[11] Writers of the Victorian age were captivated by the notion of communicating via electricity, a force or phenomenon steeped in mystery and perceived to be so ethereal as to defy physical reality. To be sure, using electricity, telegraphy could defy time and space, and when the Victorian Internet was vastly expanded from continent to continent via the submarine Atlantic Cable beginning in 1858, the effect seemed positively miraculous.

The public perception of a technological miracle bears discussion because the perception lingers to this day. Regarding the telegraph, people focused on the marvel wrought by the invisible, "medium" of electricity. The fact that this little-understood vehicle required a wire or cable infrastructure was all but ignored by the public in much the same way as the casual user of today's Internet speaks of "cyberspace," thereby ignoring a vast complex of physical infrastructure—fiber, copper, semiconducting materials, microprocessors, microcircuits, interconnecting cables and sockets and plugs, switches, and servers.

A digital network neither is nor exists in a vacuum any more than the telegraph or transcontinental cable existed in the absence of conductive materials, connectors, switches, and even wooden telegraph poles. Whether in the context of the "Victorian Internet" or of today's Internet, to ignore or evade the physical infrastructure by means of metaphors devoted to ethereal electricity or cyberspace is to fail to acknowledge the essential fragilities and vulnerabilities of both networks. Outlaws capable of ambushing a Pony Express rider were even more capable of cutting down telegraph lines and instantly disrupting the network. Those with more sophisticated nefarious purposes could also tap into the line and intercept messages or even send deliberately misleading messages of their own: "Stop the gold train at Banditville!"

When the legendary private detective Allan Pinkerton, hired to protect President-elect Abraham Lincoln on his inaugural rail journey from Springfield, Illinois, to Washington, D.C., caught wind of an assassination plot brewing among Southern sympathizers in Baltimore, he cut the telegraph lines to and from the city. He wanted to prevent conspirators from sending or receiving information on the whereabouts of the presidential train.[12] In terms of network security, this incident is revelatory: The deficiency of resilience in the telegraph network was well known to those who had reason to be in the know, even if it did not occupy a prominent place in public awareness.

As for the Atlantic Cable, remarkable though the technological achievement was, the hardware was also notoriously unreliable and subject to failure—as was to be expected with thousands of miles of spliced cable resting uneasily on the sea floor of an often-turbulent Atlantic, a vast body containing a highly corrosive, highly conductive salt solution. Eventually, issues of resilience were addressed by adding redundant wires and cabling (especially in densely populated areas) and hiring linemen to routinely inspect and maintain overground telegraph lines. As for undersea cables, these were, to the degree possible, periodically pulled up, inspected, repaired, and relaid by fleets of specially designed cable-tender ships. In the earliest days of the Atlantic Cable, transmission was extraordinarily slow. Poor reception necessitated the crudest possible form of resilience to eliminate errors: redundancy. Morse Code messages were transmitted character by character. The transmitting operator would send one character and then wait for the receiving operator to transmit it back, to confirm that it had been received without error. This back-and-forth had to be repeated until both sides of the conversation were satisfied that the single character had been properly transmitted and received. In 1858, average speed of transmission was one character per two minutes, and the first message sent took more than seventeen hours to complete.[13] Primitive, yes. But today's digital error-correction protocols share the basic principle of repeat-confirm-correct-repeat-confirm.

EXTENDING THE REACH OF DATA NETWORKING

Despite universal public acceptance of overland and undersea "wired" telegraphic communication—which was supplemented by "wired" voice communication with the emergence of the telephone (patented by Alexander Graham Bell in 1876)—there was growing awareness of the limitations imposed by the necessity of a physical infrastructure in communication networks. In response, late in the nineteenth century, a wireless networking technology began to emerge. In America, it was called radio; in Britain, more simply, wireless. On December 12, 1901, the Irish-Italian inventor

Guglielmo Marconi gave a dramatic demonstration of the potential of wireless communication by sending the first non-hardwired transatlantic message.

Not only did wireless communication technology greatly extend the reach of data networking, potentially casting an information net over the entire planet, connecting places beyond the practical reach of a physically interconnective infrastructure, it boded well for security and, therefore, network resilience. There were no wires to cut, tap, or short out. True, analog radio signals were vulnerable to deliberate interception and accidental interference, but Marconi and his associates offered a solution—what Marconi advertised as an ability to "tune [his] instruments so that no other instrument that is not similarly tuned can tap my messages."[14] So-called harmonic telegraphy was already in use for multiplexing wired messages, sending more than one message over a single telegraph wire at the same time by transmitting the messages as pulses of specific audio frequencies. A given receiving device would be tuned to the frequency of one message and not of the others. In "tuning" his wireless transmitter and receiver, Marconi adjusted the amplitude of the electromagnetic waves he produced, not the frequency of any resulting audio signal. The effect, however, was the same. If the transmitter and receiver were tuned to the same wavelength, the transmitted message would be received. If not, the message would not be received and would therefore be (Marconi claimed) secure from prying instruments and ears.

Two years after first successfully transmitting and receiving a transatlantic message, in June 1903, history's first documented attack on a wireless electronic network occurred. John Ambrose Fleming, a British physicist, was about to demonstrate long-distance radio communication before a distinguished audience at the Royal Institution, London. Three hundred miles away, in Cornwall, Fleming's employer, none other than Guglielmo Marconi, was preparing to send him a uniquely "tuned"—and therefore utterly secure—wireless signal.

The audience prepared to listen to the Morse Code message, which was acoustically amplified so that it could be heard throughout the auditorium. They waited in anticipation. Suddenly, a transmission echoed through the hall. Arthur Blok, Fleming's assistant and adept at Morse Code, instantly recognized it as the monosyllable "rats" repeated over and over. A Morse printer, which was connected to the receiver, spelled out the word as well, followed by a string of expletives and some mocking quotations from Shakespeare.

Marconi's "secure" network was intended to be a network of two and was now, unexpectedly, a network of three. Turns out it had been breached by one Nevil Maskelyne, a highly successful music hall magician by trade, who routinely used short-range wireless Morse Code transmission in his show-stopping mind-reading act. Maskelyne later explained the motive for his attack. It was, he said, an effort to expose security flaws in Marconi's design.

The Marconi incident was doubtless embarrassing, but it was hardly a deal breaker. For one thing, relatively few messages transmitted by wired or wireless telegraphy were considered matters worthy of high security. People did not routinely transmit, as they do today, personally identifiable information (PII). Business, though discussed, was not routinely executed online. If you wanted to send messages that required a high degree of security, you could always send them in secret cipher. Extremely sophisticated encryption/decryption machines have been available for a surprisingly long time. For instance, the first iteration of the legendary German "Enigma" was patented in 1918 and machines were being marketed commercially beginning in 1923.[15] Hacking to steal identities or secrets or financial information or even for fun was not common, let alone epidemic in the pre-digital era. Nevertheless, network exploits—and therefore network security—did surface as a subject of law enforcement as well as popular attention and concern even before the appearance of the personal computer and the Internet.

ACTION ITEM

Nevil Maskelyne's trolling of Marconi—his exposure of a security flaw in radio—did not, of course, kill wireless. The reason was that most people did not envision using the medium to transmit highly sensitive data. This was shortsightedness, for all that it was an instance of the reasonable prioritization of data. Digital resilience is not a one-size-fits-all approach. On the contrary, it is dynamic and depends, among other things, on reasonably assessing the security priority of different classes of data. Think of resilience as a flexible business solution, not as a moat or a high wall.

THE BIRTH OF "HACKING"

In the 1970s, people—usually young—who called themselves "phone phreaks" began almost routinely breaking into the computer networks of telephone company "exchanges" by using "blue boxes," homemade devices that synthesized the tones of a telephone operator's dialing console to do such things as switch long-distance calls.[16] Using a blue box—a youthful Steve Jobs and Steve Wozniak began their professional collaboration by marketing one they had crafted in the 1970s—a phone phreak could make free calls to just about any place in the world.[17] Truly dedicated phreakers did more than use blue boxes to make free calls—a crime known as toll fraud. They became adept at listening to touchtone tone patterns to figure out how these were used to route calls, they devoured phone company technical literature (sometimes dumpster diving to acquire such material), and they even broke into hardwired telephone equipment to wire in their own phones. A phreaker subculture developed, and some groups covertly used conference call circuits to communicate with one another in a pre-Internet version of a chat room.

During the early 1980s, the major telephone companies migrated to computerized telephone networks, which digitized dialing information and sent it separately from the audio channel via a digital channel that was inaccessible to blue boxes. This migration also signaled the emergence of the era of the personal computer, and a period in which phone phreaking morphed into what became popularly called "hacking."

To the general public, the world of computer hacking in the early 1980s was mysterious, rarefied, and fascinating. The first hacker group to be portrayed as a serious threat to network security called itself the "414s," after their Milwaukee, Wisconsin, area code. Members were indicted in 1983 for attacking some sixty mainframe computer networks, including those belonging to Los Alamos National Laboratory and the Memorial Sloan-Kettering Cancer Center.[18] The idea that "kids" could penetrate serious government and institutional networks was both upsetting and intriguing. Hackers began to achieve a certain mythic status in pop culture, as evidenced by the 1983 John Badham blockbuster *WarGames,* about a teenage "hacker," played by a young Matthew Broderick, who uses his PC and an old-school acoustic modem to connect with a military supercomputer, which he believes has given him free access to a new thermonuclear war simulation game. In fact, he nearly starts World War III.[19]

Within about three years of the 414s and *WarGames,* the popular perception of hacking had escalated from a pop-culture phenomenon to an increasingly serious law enforcement concern. Amid a growing frequency and volume of network breaches, Congress passed the Computer Fraud and Abuse Act in 1986, giving law enforcement and the courts jurisdiction over digital attackers. During the late 1980s and throughout the 1990s, breaches and other security incidents became more and more common.

The public often seemed to regard hacking as a form of social expression rather than as a criminal enterprise. Figures like Kevin Mitnick attained the stature of a cyber Billy the Kid. At sixteen, Mitnick had breached the computer system of Digital Equipment Corporation (DEC) and copied advanced DEC operating system software. Nine years later, in 1988, he was convicted for that crime and sentenced to a year in prison followed by three years of supervised release. Before his probation ended, he breached voicemail computers belonging to Pacific Bell, and then went on the lam, breaching dozens of computer networks while he was a fugitive. Arrested early in 1995, he confessed to wire fraud, computer fraud, and intercepting a wire communication, for which he served a total of five years in prison. Presumably responding to the absence of public outrage over Mitnick's exploits, law enforcement officials argued to the sentencing judge that the hacker was capable of starting a thermonuclear war simply by whistling the launch code for NORAD missiles into a prison payphone. The judge took this seriously, and Mitnick spent eight months of his term in solitary confinement for fear he would get to a phone and start World War III.[20]

Less well publicized during this period were attacks even more consequential for their impact on network security. In 1988, for example, four men were arrested for breaching the computer system of the First National Bank of Chicago in a foiled attempt to transfer $70 million to Austrian bank accounts.[21] This incident certainly roiled the banking and business communities, but it was the emergence that same year of a piece of malware specifically designed to penetrate, compromise, and exploit networks that prompted the federal government to create the Computer Emergency Response Team (CERT) at Pittsburgh's Carnegie Mellon University. Moreover, CERT operated under the direction of the Defense Advanced Research Agency (DARPA), the very Department of Defense agency that had funded the creation of ARPANET, the direct precursor of the Internet itself.[22]

The item of malware in question was the so-called Morris worm. Now, in the late 1980s, the public's hands-on experience with computing and networked computing was still new. What everybody did understand quite clearly, however, was the concept of embezzlement, particularly when the funds at risk were potentially one's own. The idea of a digital "worm" was harder to grasp. People understood that computers could be broken into, but they had to be educated about the means through which malware was propagated on a computer network so that it could infect any number of machines on that network. Once this notion was explained, however imperfectly, there was considerable fear concerning the stealthy power of a network worm to steal information and other assets like the proverbial thief in the night.

Cornell University student Robert Tappan Morris, the worm's namesake and creator, never intended to do harm. He was neither a criminal nor even a quasi-recreational hacker. His purpose in creating the worm (he claimed) was to exploit weak passwords and vulnerabilities in widely used Unix operating systems so that he could "worm" his way across the entire Internet as a way of gauging its size—which was not all that vast in the late 1980s. The Morris worm was essentially an early network monitoring—or at least estimating—tool. It was an attempt to create some portion of the picture of Internet topology. The unintended consequence of this exercise in cyber census taking was a large-scale distributed denial of service (DDoS) attack. Morris coded his worm in a way that it might infect the same computer over and over again, with each process slowing the machine down. Eventually, networked computers became too slow to function.

The damage caused by the Morris worm was important for both the public and professional perception of the threat to networks during this period. For this exploit was not computer-aided theft, something that is easily comprehended. It was an attack on the functionality of a digital network that people were just beginning to rely on. The Morris worm infected an estimated 6,000 major Unix machines—about 10 percent of the 60,000 computers connected to the Internet at the time. The raw numbers are small because the Internet was small, but the fraction of the network affected was huge.

The lessons of the Morris worm were nevertheless highly useful. First, the creation of CERT demonstrated the government's understanding that the digital network was becoming an issue of national security and therefore required the resources of the national government to help protect and defend it. Second, the nature of the attack, an exploitation of inherent vulnerabilities in Unix code, revealed that *network* security depended at some level on *software* security. This meant engineering software to avoid introducing vulnerabilities in the first place—engineering software to be secure by design. If the Unix vulnerabilities had not existed, Morris could not have created his worm. But developers are human. They will make mistakes or simply fail to recognize all vulnerabilities.

Efforts at prevention therefore need to be supplemented by continuous monitoring of networks to detect attacks as well as their impact. Monitoring enables a rapid response to breaches and attempted breaches, and provides information useful for enhancing the security of the underlying software. Resilience is a continuous endeavor.

A BRIEF HISTORY OF NETWORK SECURITY

Threats have always been a part of networks, both analog and digital. Typically, security has lagged behind the emergence of threats. CERT was established to promote the security of the United States' rapidly growing national digital network. That was admirable. Unfortunately, CERT also established a model of a reactive rather than a preemptive approach to computer and network security. The result of this was the proliferation of viruses and other malware throughout the 1980s and 1990s, each pursued by an antivirus software "cure."

Indeed, the first wave of "digital security" became largely defined as the detection and removal of malware from computers. A profitable antivirus industry (on the order of $6 billion to $8 billion today) was born, and relatively little effort was devoted either to designing security into software code or developing effective ways to monitor increasingly large and complex digital networks. Unsurprisingly, the 1990s became a decade of exploits that exposed security gaps in numerous high-profile corporate and government systems, ranging from Griffiss Air Force Base, to NASA, to the Korean Atomic Research Institute. An attack against the AT&T network brought down its long-distance service for a time, and the U.S. Department of Defense recorded a quarter-million attacks against its own computers and networks in 1995 alone.

That same year, the Computer Security Institute determined that one in five websites had been hacked.[23]

If government and corporate systems were the targets of choice during the 1990s, the rise of Internet e-commerce introduced a profit motive and a vastly heightened degree of interactive access that brought explosive growth in malicious attacks. In the opening decades of the twenty-first century, computer networks more and more frequently became the targets of the kind of organized crime breaches—sometimes state-sponsored or at least state-sanctioned—described in Chapter 1.

Hyper-connectivity created a new economy and a new threat landscape. Time and again, the vulnerability of code was exposed. Sometimes the weak point was in software; sometimes in the firmware (software embedded in engineered products and systems) of such Internet of Things devices as point-of-sale (POS) credit card readers. The government and industry responded, to be sure, but not always by focusing on building security into software design. True, as early as the 1970s, three Massachusetts Institute of Technology (MIT) graduates innovated a code solution by creating RSA encryption technology, which later found its way into the likes of Microsoft Windows and such popular applications as the Quicken check writing and banking application.[24] Network encryption-based security approaches accompanied the rise of the Internet, most notably the development of virtual private network (VPN) technology, Secure Sockets Layer (SSL), Secure Electronic Transactions (SET), and Data Encryption Standard (DES). All enhanced network security, as did antivirus software and firewalls. IT professionals operating large networks turned to Intrusion Detection Systems (IDS), content filtering software, the separation of vital components of operating systems, and behavior analysis software as bulwarks to defend their networks.

Yet the network guardians kept playing catch-up. In 2007, then governor of Arizona (and, later, secretary of Homeland Security in the Obama administration) Janet Napolitano scoffed at the idea of building a wall along the U.S.–Mexican border. "I declared a state of emergency and was the first governor to openly advocate for the National Guard at the border," she told the National Press Club in 2007, "yet, I also have refused to agree that a wall by itself is an answer. As I often say, 'You show me a 50-foot wall, and I'll show you a 51-foot ladder.'"[25] This quip might well be used to describe the apparent spirit in which attackers view each new defensive IT obstacle—never as a disincentive to attempt a breach, but as a fresh challenge to be overcome. Despite rising IT security budgets, 2016 was a banner year for major—sometimes spectacular—breaches. The nonprofit Identity Theft Resource Center (ITRC) reported 845 total breaches in its banking/credit/financial, business/educational, government/military, and medical/healthcare categories, representing the compromise of 29,765,131 records.[26]

HOW THE SHIFT FROM DIGITAL SYSTEMS OF RECORD TO SYSTEMS OF ENGAGEMENT OUTRAN CYBERSECURITY

Before the rise of the Internet, computer systems were primarily systems of record. They stored data and made it available for retrieval and interaction on a scale limited to a given network, which had few connections to the world beyond it. For such systems, a Maginot Line approach to security—a digital wall or line of firewall and software fortifications defending and protecting a perimeter—was appropriate as well as reasonably effective. Perimeter protection evolved into the second wave of cybersecurity strategy and survives today primarily as the network firewall. To the extent that the computer was a physical machine isolated from other machines or connected only to trusted machines and trusted users, the main security concerns were protecting the physical equipment and preventing some intruder or a rogue insider from uploading malicious software or downloading valuable data via a floppy disk. This was *computer* security rather than *network* security, and it became inadequate with the explosive growth of the Internet, which meant that most computer systems had morphed from systems of record to systems of engagement, decentralized and open to peer interactions. No longer were security strategies modeled on physical-world scenarios sufficient to maintain complete security, although this method of intrusion prevention accounts for about $20 billion in security products sold worldwide.

ACTION ITEM

One way to understand the need for resilience in addition to security is to recognize that the way we use computers has changed from devices that primarily create records to devices that mostly engage with other devices. When computers were used mainly as calculators, financial ledgers, employee information files, and the like, vaultlike security was imperative and sufficient. Now that we use intensively interconnected computers to interact with other intensively connected computers, security is still necessary but by no means sufficient. Today, we must assume that security measures will be sooner or later penetrated because we are all exposed. For this reason, active measures of resilience are necessary to allow networks to continue to operate while breaches are contained.

The pre-Internet era was analogous to the situation on the Western Front in World War I (1914–1918), which was fought along a demarcated, relatively static line of physical trenches. More recent wars, beginning with the Vietnam War of the 1960s and 1970s, have been fought on multiple and typically fluid "fronts." In fact, the word and concept of a *front* is meaningless in such wars. The web-based, cloud-oriented, intensively interactive networked systems that characterize the modern computing landscape likewise present no single front or perimeter to defend. It is often impossible to distinguish clearly and cleanly between "trusted" and "untrusted" computers. Firewalls are important, but they won't stop an insider from thoughtlessly clicking on a toxic link in a phishing email. Besides, the value of most networks in an era of engagement is in who they include, not who they exclude. A dynamic security strategy begins with inherently secure software and firmware design.

The resilience of a physical structure depends on the resilience of the individual components with which it is built. The resilience of an organization depends on the individual resilience of its members. The resilience of a digital network begins with software and firmware elements that are inherently designed to be secure. Of course, it is not enough simply to aggregate resilient elements. Resilient elements connected poorly do not create a resilient network, not in a digital system and not in a corporate or institutional system. Even resilient people make mistakes, whether they are building a digital network or designing an organization.

Software security is necessary to network security, but it is not sufficient to it. There is a wider danger, which may be summed up in a warning issued by the FBI back in 2012. According to Gregory S. Saikin of the Baker Hostetler law firm, the FBI warned users of Internet-based social networking websites that hackers, "ranging from con artists to foreign government spies," trolled for the purpose of exploiting "the users' identifying and related personal information." The FBI report explained that these social networking hackers were "carrying out two general tactics, which are often combined." They acted as "social engineers," exploiting personal connections through social networks, and they wrote and manipulated software code "to gain access or install unwanted software on your computer or phone."

The FBI warned that the "hackers are impersonating social networking users with the intent to target the user's workplace." The favored tactic, the FBI pointed out, was "spear phishing," in which an attacker sends an email that appears to be from a trusted or known source and of interest to the targeted user. The email typically contains a hyperlink or an executable file. When the victim clicks on the link or opens the file, a malware program is installed in the target's computer. Depending on the nature and function of the malware, the assault might provide the hacker access to the firm's data, including (for example) trade secrets, security measures, employee files, or, in the case of the attacks on Target Corporation, credit card data.[27]

Most successful attacks on computer networks use Trojan horses that are introduced into the network through spear phishing emails or messages. No matter how sophisticated the particular malware program is, it is almost always inert—harmless—until a human being opens the phishing email and clicks on whatever link or attachment it offers. Thus, the second stage of a network attack almost always depends on social engineering to get started. That is, a human being has to be persuaded to open the gate, admitting the Trojan horse into walled Troy.

Savvy computer users and those working for savvy networked organizations are often quite aware of and sophisticated about spear phishing emails. They are not easily duped. But, sooner or later, an extremely good spear phishing exploit will overcome the healthy, educated, and practiced skepticism of even the savviest user. Hillary Clinton's presidential campaign manager John Podesta fell victim to a "spear-phishing hack . . . instigated with an email that purported to come from Google informing him that someone had used his password to try to access his Google account. It included a link to a spoofed Google webpage that asked him to change his password because his current password had been stolen." What happened next was the collision of human error with digital technology. An aide to Podesta did precisely the right thing, immediately forwarding the suspicious email to the Clinton campaign's IT staff to ask if it was legitimate. A staffer, Charles Delavan, replied that it was a "legitimate e-mail" and that Podesta should "change his password immediately." The thing is, Delavan had meant to type "illegitimate," but had left out the "il." Thanks to this typo, Podesta gave his password to the Russian-based hacker "Fancy Bear and his emails began appearing on WikiLeaks in early October."[28] Increasingly adept and persuasive efforts at social engineering combined with dogged persistence, not technical innovation in the craft of malware creation, have made recent attacks particularly damaging. Add the mindset of today's most dedicated hackers—a mindset that embraces organized crime as a business model—then stir in the inexhaustible abundance of credulous human fallibility, and you have a recipe for network vulnerability, regardless of what level and combination of hardware and software defenses are used. Innovation and the human factor render every network intensely dynamic, with too many moving parts to defend with absolute certainty. The only alternative is to build in resilience that will absorb an attack and contain it while providing a sufficient level of reliable service and uninterrupted connectivity to allow the enterprise to continue operating while under attack.

ACTION ITEMS

Spear phishing is an attack that comes via an email that appears to be from an individual or business you know and therefore trust. It is a con that exploits that trust to get credit card and bank account numbers, passwords, and financial information on your computer and computers networked with you. Your network is only as resilient as the least resilient individual connected to it; therefore, educate everyone on your network to do the following:

- Think before clicking on any email attachment.
- Understand that attackers can persuasively mimic emails from legitimate organizations, corporations, and individuals with whom you have a relationship.
- Learn how to use the features of your email client (the program you use to access your email) so that you can see the true origin of an email. Better yet, find out how to set your client to show you this automatically. If "Your Bank" shows up in the email header, but something else shows up in the actual address (xyz@123.com, etc.), you know that you are being phished.
- Skilled spear phishers use social media and other sources to learn your name and to discover companies and organizations with whom you do business. The attacker may even know that you made a recent purchase and may refer to it. This knowledge is often reflected in the content of the email.
- Do not be lulled by familiarity. Resist the impulse to click on a button or hyperlink. Instead, use your browser to go directly to the company (bank, partner firm, etc.) the email purports to be from. Check for messages there.

- Do not reply to the email. Do not furnish any information requested. Instead, use your browser to go directly to the organization that the email purports to be from.
- Report phishing emails to your organization's IT or digital security manager.
- Guard your personally identifiable information (PII). Audit your online presence. What kind of information do you disclose on the social web? Your name? Email address? Friends' and colleagues' names? Friends' and colleagues' email addresses? What kinds of personal and professional information do you disclose in your posts? Assume an attacker will gain access to all of this.
- Audit your passwords. Don't make them easy to figure out. Don't use the same password for multiple accounts. Change passwords frequently.

HOW DECENTRALIZATION CAN ENHANCE RESILIENCE

Resilience is a necessary strategy, but it does have limits. Resilient network architectures built on firmware and software elements designed with security as a high priority can usually be counted on to reduce the impact of attacks. Scanning tools identify vulnerabilities in software, and modeling tools diagnose weakness in network architecture. Monitoring tools detect unusual activity that may indicate that an attack or breach is in progress. Used in combination, such tools help us to design, build, and maintain resilient digital networks. An internal network may operate with a considerable degree of central control; however, the hallmark of the Internet, the vast external network to which most enterprise systems of engagement are connected, is decentralization. As noted in Chapter 1, security expert Richard A. Clarke points out that the earliest architects of the Internet, back in the ARPANET days, "did not want [the Internet] to be controlled by governments, either singly or collectively, and so they designed a system that placed a higher priority on decentralization than on security."[29] Clarke sees this as an inherent source of weakness, making it difficult to provide adequate protection to a network of nodes that, while interconnected, are also independent of one another. Yet if decentralization is a source of insecurity, it is also a source of resilience in that it denies attackers the opportunity to strike a fatally decapitating blow.

The decentralized Internet has sometimes made non-digital "real-world" networks more resilient. For example, by enabling coordination of individual action while simultaneously allowing decentralized leadership, the Internet has made some popular political movements less vulnerable to a decapitating attack by the forces of a repressive central government. A case-in-point often cited is the 2010 "Jasmine Revolution" in Tunisia, widely credited with igniting the Arab Awakening or Arab Spring. In 2011, journalist Colin Delany reported on a discussion at National Public Radio's Washington, D.C., headquarters led by a young Tunisian protester named Rim Nour.[30] Nour was a Tunisian whose background combined technology and public policy. He told the NPR audience that social media did not foment the Jasmine Revolution, but did accelerate it and, even more important, helped Tunisians organize and maintain it. By 2010, many Tunisians were enthusiastic users of Internet technology, and 85 percent of the population owned cellphones. Some 2 million of the country's 10 million residents and an additional 2 million Tunisian expats were on Facebook at the start of the Jasmine Revolution.

Although Western journalists sometimes called the Jasmine Revolution the "Twitter Revolution," Twitter had a tiny footprint in Tunisia during 2010. No more than 500 Twitter accounts were active in the country. Yet those Tunisians who did tweet were avid and skilled political activists quite capable of leveraging their Twitter presence in ways that produced a social impact highly disproportionate to the small number of users. The Tunisian government could do little to suppress cellphone use, but it did exercise censorship control over YouTube and other major Internet social media channels.

Nour explained that the Jasmine Revolution was sparked by the response to the self-immolation of Mohamed Bouazizi, a street merchant in the rural town of Sidi Bouzid. On December 17, 2010, when a policewoman seized the unlicensed vegetable cart by which Bouazizi eked out a living for himself and his family, Bouazizi appealed to local officials. Rebuffed by them, Bouazizi doused himself with an unidentified flammable liquid and set himself ablaze—just outside of the municipal building where he had pleaded his case in vain.

Bouazizi's act of self-immolation was not captured on cellphone video, but the brutal police response to the subsequent demonstrations was. Activists shared the videos not only within Tunisia, but throughout the region and the world. In the West, the footage was picked up by major broadcast news networks. As protests developed across Tunisia, leaders organized what Western commentators called "smart mobs," creating a political movement coordinated via cellphones and Facebook. The demonstrations gathered so much momentum that Tunisian president Zine El Abidine Ben Ali fled the country. At this, the revolution threatened to tip into violent anarchy, which was reined in by social media appeals that counteracted rumors and promoted disciplined organization. The entire drama was shared online with the world, and the global response was, in turn, transmitted back to the Tunisian demonstrators via social media.

Belatedly, the Ben Ali government launched a media counter-offensive via the television and radio networks it controlled. This demonstration of central power, however, proved to be no match for decentralized social media, which poked holes in government lies. When, for instance, government TV broadcast a pro-Ben Ali demonstration, Jasmine activists posted on Facebook their video footage revealing how few supporters Ben Ali actually had. The decentralized Internet facilitated the exchange of information among activists and made it possible to respond to real-world social and political developments in real-time. Mobile video technology and the Internet, especially as connected to conventional broadcast media worldwide, gave the Jasmine Revolution global exposure.

Tragically, the Tunisian experience of a successful and productive revolution proved to be the exception during the next few years of Middle East turmoil. The same Internet whose decentralization outmaneuvered the tyranny of a repressive central government enabled organizations like al-Qaeda and the Islamic State (or ISIS) to recruit and motivate, at times even coordinate, the actions of terrorists across the globe. The decentralization capable of defeating a despotic government also defies the efforts of democratic governments to locate the sources of recruitment and direction or to identify individual recruits to terror. Certainly, the individualized, interactive nature of networked communication prevents simply shutting down the network in a bid to interrupt terrorist recruitment and other plotting.

HOW DECENTRALIZATION CAN DIMINISH RESILIENCE

The decentralized architecture of the Internet, together with the ability even relatively unsophisticated hackers possess to use off-the-shelf software and web solutions to spoof Internet addresses, makes tracing threats back across the net extremely difficult. When epidemiologists investigate an outbreak of disease, they always begin by attempting to identify "patient number one," the initial source of infection. It is a difficult but feasible task. In the case of digital networks, the difficulty of finding the original perpetrator of, say, a breach or a DDoS attack is compounded by the attacker's ability to connect through large numbers of network nodes, to spoof points of origin, and even to enlist the aid of governments and government-related institutions willing to help mask the source of an attack.

Those whose responsibility it is to serve as guardians of enterprise or government networks continually find themselves outgunned when it comes to preventing attacks. When an attack hits, they do possess certain forensic tools and techniques to determine—or at least guess at—the source of an attack. The breach of the Democratic National Committee in 2016 and the WikiLeaks disclosure of emails and other materials embarrassing to Democratic presidential candidate Hillary Clinton and others bore forensic hallmarks of other attacks by Russian state-sponsored hackers.[31] Yet, as of this writing, no direct means of remediation or retaliation precisely targeting a specific set of hackers could be found. The victims and law enforcement have almost no practical recourse. Besides, the damage was done by the time credible theories of the sources of the attacks had even emerged. As a practical matter, the most that could have been done to defend against the breach was to have monitored the DNC's presumably far-flung networks with tools capable of showing the dynamic typology of the networks and the traffic flow across them. This might well have enabled a timely, agile, and resilient response to minimize the volume of the material exfiltrated. As we know from other major breaches, such as the attack on Target discussed in Chapter 1, both infiltration and exfiltration during an exploit take a considerable amount of time and generate a detectable, if not obvious, level of activity.

HOW NETWORK KNOWLEDGE BUILDS NETWORK RESILIENCE

Tools that model your network, showing how the bad guys can get into your systems and where they can go once they have infiltrated them, tools that light up the paths to your most critical assets, enhance your knowledge of your network. Software that provides this level of insight can buy you the time you need to contain an intrusion and prevent exfiltration, minimizing its immediate impact so that you can stay in operation even as you work to remove the threat. The better you can prevent an attack, or contain or interrupt an incident, the smaller you make any post-breach data compromise.

There is no sovereign strategy against breach or shipwreck except severing connectivity or remaining ashore. In network parlance, that would be "air gapping" the network. No operator of a system of engagement can unplug, any more than a sailor can remain beached. Fortunately, there are practical means, whether you manage a network or handle a ship, of increasing and maintaining a level of resilience sufficient to spare you all or some damage or loss in the event of a mishap. This has always been true of networks and ships. In the case of networks, however, it has never been a more urgent truth than it is today.

TAKEAWAY

Resilience is a matter of reducing the volume and severity of damage and loss as well as staying in business or on mission. In such a reduction is the possibility not only of survival and recovery, but even of continuing to operate without interruption. In an intensively networked civilization "of fibrous, threadlike, wiry, stringy, ropy, capillary character,"[32] in which digital and non-digital networks interface at so many points—trillions, perhaps—connectivity is power. The catch is that connectivity is also a threat. The ship allows you to set sail, even as it exposes you to the possibility of shipwreck.

4

DIGITALLY BOUND

Getting the C-Suite and Board Up to Speed on Digital Resilience

***We are* Homo dictyous,** a networking species. In recent years, the most important networks that bind our global civilization have been digital, and each new digital network is increasingly extensive, interconnecting more and more aspects of our lives. Nevertheless, despite its ubiquity—or maybe because of it—for most of us, the mechanism of digital interconnectivity remains a black box. Data goes in, the products of data come out, and who knows what lies between? Not many. A cadre of engineers, a handful of IT managers, and far fewer executives. This chapter is a primer—for executives and other organizational leaders—on the digital networks that all at once bind, liberate, enable, and endanger us.

Do executives and board members really want such a primer? I have met many who say they do and who have even asked me where they can find one. But the more significant question is not one of desire, but of need. We are far beyond the days when a digital network was an adjunct to business, a convenient alternative to walking down the hallway with a floppy disk to share with a colleague five cubicles down and three across. Today, networks are not only integral to business, they are in large measure the very substance of business. Networks enable many vital business functions, bring to light as well as fruition myriad opportunities, and, yes, expose the enterprise to grave risk.

Networks must no longer be the exclusive province of IT. They are the one element of corporate infrastructure that embraces the entire business. No manager, executive, or board member can afford to think of the network as a "box" of any kind, let alone a *black box,* about which it is fitting and proper for the C-suite and boardroom to be totally ignorant. Everyone with a guiding stake in the business should have a foundational understanding of digital networks.

WHAT IS A NETWORK?

Let us begin at the analog level. Seat three people at a conference table, and you have the basis of a network. Seems simple. But you cannot move from the elements of a network to a functioning network without first addressing three functional requirements:

1. Ensuring that the nodes of the network can hear one another.
2. Ensuring that they speak a mutually intelligible language.
3. Ensuring that they have one conversation at a time and do not speak over one another.

The first requirement is usually easy to meet. Seating the participants at a conference table brings them close enough to be heard—unless it is a very large conference table in a noisy room, or one or more participants suffers from, say, significant hearing loss. Even so, such problems can be overcome by straightforward measures—get a smaller table, silence the noise, amplify the sound for those with hearing deficits, or if necessary, include a qualified sign language interpreter in the meeting.

As for the second requirement, the necessity for a mutually intelligible language, this does not always call for any special preparation. In many (most of the time, most) situations, everyone speaks the same language by default. Nevertheless, if a language barrier exists, qualified translators can be included in the meeting.

Finally, the third requirement: There is nothing built into the biological structure of the human organism that prevents people from speaking simultaneously and thereby rendering meaningful verbal communication difficult, if not impossible. All that prevents the jabber of crosstalk is socialization that usually begins early in childhood. We learn the "polite" convention of speaking in turn and of asking questions and responding to them. For the most part, in adult life and business, the convention is applied effectively, except in heated exchanges, where network participants holler over each other. When this happens, meaningful communication threatens to break down.

The elementary networking of in-person meetings requires a manageable number of participants, their physical proximity, their command of a common language, and reasonably good manners. Of these requirements, the absence of physical proximity may be readily overcome by technology. If one of the three participants is in another room, we might install an intercom. Things get more complicated if *each* participant is in a different room, however. For the sake of this discussion, let's assume that only wired intercom technology is available. We would have to equip each participant with an intercom unit (a transceiver, complete with a microphone and a speaker and therefore capable of both transmission and reception) and run wires connecting each unit with each of the others. For a network of three nodes, this means that each unit would need three sets of wires, for a total (3 times 3) of nine sets of wires. This arrangement solves the lack of proximity, but it puts something of a strain on the requirement that the participants speak in turn. Without the visual cues available in face-to-face networks, the risk of talking over one another is multiplied.

TELEPHONY: FROM ANALOG TO DIGITAL VOICE NETWORKING

The word *telephone* is a compound of the Greek *tele,* meaning "afar," and *phone,* meaning "sound" or "voice." The invention of the telephone enabled networking without the necessity of proximity. It enabled networking over distances. Indeed, the earliest telephone service used a system that resembled what we've just imagined for a conversation among people in different rooms, namely microphones and speakers connected by wires. The catch is that, in telephony's early days, multiplexing, the simultaneous transmission and reception of multiple messages along a single line, was severely limited. Yet it was also impossible to string separate wires between every pair of telephones. For this reason, a key component in early telephone networks was a human being called the *operator.* Everyone who had a telephone was wired to a central office in which a team—often a large team—of operators worked. Each telephone had a single connection to the operator, whose job it was to connect, at a plugboard called a switchboard, your outgoing call to the correct target telephone. When you were finished speaking, the operator would pull out the connection on the switchboard, and your call was terminated—disconnected.

The central telephone office, where the operators worked, was the hub of each telephone network. In the early days, wire connected each telephone to the central office. The range of the network under this system was limited to the radius within which a set of telephone subscribers lived or worked. If you wanted to make a call to a more distant phone, a phone beyond the circle covered by your central office, you had to rely on your operator to relay your call to the next central station, which would relay it to the next, until you had reached the central office that was connected to the caller you were attempting to reach. Such long-distance calls could be relayed through many central offices, depending on how far away your target phone was. Within a given area, the number of wires carried on a telephone pole was relatively limited, since individual homes and businesses were connected to the nearest pole, and everything was transmitted to and from the central office. The long-distance wires were more numerous than the local wires, since the calls had to be carried between central offices on many separate wires. Indeed, in the early days of telephone communication during the late nineteenth century and early twentieth, the number of wires on the poles was equal to the number of long-distance calls the system could simultaneously carry.

Long-distance telephone communication required a heavy investment in copper wire and was therefore expensive. Your call meant that one "line" (wire) was being used and was therefore unavailable for other callers; therefore, the telephone company charged handsomely for long-distance, billing callers by the minute or even fraction of a minute. This was partly an effort to collect sufficient revenue and partly to get one caller off the line as quickly as possible, so that the next customer could get on.

The early telephone networks had more in common with in-person conversational networks than with the digital networks of today. Those early networks were controlled by human beings (operators), and the "protocols" governing them more closely resemble the age-old social protocols of polite conversation ("wait your turn") than they do the automated, software-dependent communication protocols of today's digital networking. From the user's perspective, the early telephone networks were so easy to understand that no one gave much thought to them—unless something like a storm knocked down a few poles, bringing down some wires.

In the 1960s, telephone companies began to evolve toward digital technology, replacing electromechanical switching systems with electronic switching. The companies also automated most control features, reducing and eventually eliminating the need for human operators. Most important, electronic switching evolved into digital telephony, in which (among other things) voice signals are digitized so that many, many more calls can be handled on a single line. In other words, digitization greatly increased the bandwidth of the telephone network. This created a profound revolution in technology, but it was also a largely invisible revolution. People had to get accustomed to pushing buttons instead of fingering rotary dials, to punching in numbers-only phone numbers instead of dialing alphanumeric ones, and to "direct dialing" long-distance numbers by "area codes" instead of connecting through the "long-distance operator." None of this required radically reeducating the phone-using public. As for the telephone networks, which had been extensively transformed, ordinary callers did not need to know anything about them. They picked up their phones, punched in a number, and the thing just worked. End of story.

And "network security"? Anyone who ever read a detective novel or paid attention during Nixon's Watergate scandal knew that it was possible to tap or bug a phone. Many people understood that telephonic eavesdropping could be done by physically planting a device in the receiver of a target's phone, by splicing into the line going into a building, or even by setting up a listening post integrated into the network. But most people believed—quite correctly—that they would never be targeted for bugging, whether by criminals or law enforcement. Gangsters, spies, and crooked politicians were bugged, not ordinary people. Besides, extracting useful information via telephone eavesdropping was labor-intensive and time-consuming. Generally, covert human monitors had to spend hundreds of hours listening to banal conversations before they hit intelligence pay dirt. And most taps never yielded anything of importance. So, even from the point of view of security, few telephone users paid any attention to the network. In truth, they had no reason to do so.

ACTION ITEM

Digital networks have exponentially multiplied the power of networking. With the massively increased communication and business opportunities have come massively increased personal and business risks. These, in turn, impose significant new responsibilities on the users of our communications and computing networks. Most important: Each of us has to learn enough about how networks operate—and, specifically, how our particular networks are structured—to make informed and effective decisions concerning digital security. The responsibility to learn is part of the price we pay for the benefits of the technology of global digital connectivity.

HOW COMPUTER NETWORKS GOT TO BE THE WAY THEY ARE

Telephone communication started out as people conversing with people through a device that carried voices from afar. The telephone was an instrument, nothing more. In fact, for most people, it lay unused more than it was used. They called. They talked. They hung up. And they went about their day. This is quite different from the way we employ computer-based communication. Even though we use computers and computer programs to communicate with one another, it is the computers, not we human beings, that communicate over the network. What is more, computers are generally much more active than telephones. Whenever a networked computer is on, it sends brief messages to determine if some other computer systems are online, and it responds to such messages sent by other computers. If software programs such as an email client or instant messaging software are online, the computer will receive emails and messages, whether a human user is present or not. Many common computer programs work quietly behind the scenes, communicating online whether we are at the keyboard or not. And many computers are left online 24/7.

The full range of computer activity on networks is extensive, from exchanges of very brief messages, to data of intermediate length, to massive uploads or downloads of complex software programs, huge databases, or streamed digitized video. In short, the traffic on any computer or network of computers is continual and varied. The explosion of networked "smart" devices—from thermostats to monitoring and alarm systems—has put billions (perhaps already trillions) of special-purpose computers online across the Internet of Things (IoT). Yet while there may or may not be human beings personally creating the data in any given "conversation" among our many networked machines, there must always be a network.

Networking in the earliest days of connecting computers looked more like early telephone networking than it resembled today's digital networks. Basically, two machines were connected by wires. Communication was serial. Each item or message was sent complete and, after one was uploaded complete, the next one was sent complete. Software automated the data queue, or a human operator could create data or retrieve it from storage and send it. Simple one-to-one networking could be done between two computers in the same building or in adjacent buildings by running wires between them. When connecting computers in different buildings but, say, within the same city, the most convenient networking solution was to lease existing wires from telephone companies. If your business involved a great deal of data exchange, you arranged with the telephone company for an always-on connection, which simply meant that the end of your line was connected at the central phone office to the end of the line that went to the outside world.

If you wanted to send data or messages only occasionally, you did not need to lease a line, but used your existing telephone service. You installed a modem (*mo*dulator-*dem*odulator) between your computer and your telephone connection to modulate the carrier wave signals of the POTS ("plain old telephone system") to encode digital information from the computer into analog signals capable of transmission over ordinary analog phone lines. The modem wired to the computer on the receiving end would demodulate the analog signal, converting it back to a digital format usable by a computer. The earliest modems were acoustic. They had no wired connection to the telephone network. Instead, the user would lift the handset off the cradle of her telephone and place it on the modem, which had a microphone to accommodate the microphone (mouth) part of the handset and a speaker to accommodate the receiver (ear) part. In this way, an instrument intended to be applied to the human ear and brought up next to the human mouth became a wireless computer interface. Because neither the uploading nor the downloading computer was always online, a human being at the uploading computer would telephone a human being at the downloading computer to tell that "operator" to turn on her machine and her modem and prepare to receive an upload.

The drawbacks of as-needed modem computer transmission were that it was relatively slow, that its relatively narrow bandwidth limited the size of data items that could be transmitted, that it was subject to interference and corruption by analog "line noise" and other transmission problems, and that it required human intervention to coordinate the activity of the machines. The drawback of the always-on, leased line arrangement was that it was expensive. If you needed to lease long-distance lines, it could be *very* expensive. But the biggest drawback of both the on-demand and always-on approaches was being limited to one-on-one communication. Clearly, something more practical, flexible, and affordable was required if computers were to communicate in more generally collaborative ways.

At the end of the 1960s and into the early 1980s, two networking concepts emerged to address the demand for affordable collaboration among computers widely distributed across the United States and the world. First, researchers in various universities who wanted to collaborate more fully by routinely sending each other messages and data via their computers worked out an alternative to leasing very costly long-distance telephone lines. They created relays of local computers. Computer B would accept an upload from computer A across town and relay the data to computer C not too far away in the next town, and so on. The network chain could be made as long as needed to get the data where it had to go. Now, this relay arrangement was not *exactly* a simple bucket brigade. Pre-Internet bandwidth was narrow, so when computer A's message reached computer B, it would usually have to wait behind other messages in a queue before it could be sent on to computer C, where (unless computer C was the final destination) it would almost certainly be placed at the back of another queue to await transmission to computer D. Computer operators participating in the chain had to agree to store and forward messages, and so these first long-distance digital networks were called store-and-forward networks. It was a very simple network architecture, and it was both a great advance beyond overland mailing or shipping and much cheaper, as well as being more flexible than leasing a long-distance line.

THE INTERNET: WHO NEEDED IT?

While university research departments made do with their store-and-forward networks, the U.S. Department of Defense decided that it could not depend on a means of digital data communications that was not only slow (and often slow over an unpredictably variable range), but also highly vulnerable both to spontaneous failure and to enemy attack. Indeed, the entire telephone network was vulnerable, and the Department of Defense wanted to create a secure—as well as resilient—communications network alternative to the whole thing. Accordingly, the department's Advanced Research Projects Agency (ARPA) funded a combination of university and tech firm researchers to design and build a rapid and robust network for civilian contractors and military personnel to collaborate on defense-related research. The result, in 1969, was

ARPANET, the first digital network that implemented a common addressing system and protocol called TCP/IP—Transmission Control Protocol/Internet Protocol.

TCP/IP was a foundational breakthrough in digital networking. It was—and remains—a protocol suite that specifies uniform standards for end-to-end data transmission, including how data should be addressed, transmitted, routed, and received. Most important of all was the concept of packetization, or packet switching, which TCP/IP also codified. The ARPANET scientists realized that the most efficient way to move data across a network with many relays (called "hops") was most certainly not repeatedly storing and forwarding whole messages. Instead, if each message was broken into pieces—into data "packets" of uniform short length—and the packets sent individually, entire messages could move along much faster. Instead of a whole short message having to wait for a whole long message to complete transmission, the first packet of the short message needed to wait only until the current packet of the large message had been transmitted. By breaking messages into packets of a standardized length, data could be sent continuously over the network, in a receive-and-send rhythm instead of a time-consuming receive-and-store-and-forward sequence. What had been stop-and-go traffic came to resemble more of a continuous flow.

Not only did packet switching save valuable time, it saved storage space, which was even more valuable (because it was so costly) in early digital computers. (In 1980, the cost to store a gigabyte of data was between $193,000 and $770,000; by 2009, as low as $0.07.[1]) Thanks to packet switching, instead of having to store an entire message from computer A possibly for hours before computer B could relay the message to computer C, computer B only needed to store a few packets for a matter of seconds while they waited their turn on the link to computer C.

While ARPANET was being built, the National Science Foundation (NSF) created a similar and parallel network called NSFNet. In 1981, NSFNet was largely combined with ARPANET and, at length, NSF took over much of the ARPANET TCP/IP technology, establishing a more widely distributed "network of networks" capable of handling much more traffic. NSF called this super-network the "Internet."

In the meantime, as networks abandoned store-and-forward to embrace TCP/IP and packet switching, new hardware was developed, specialized computers dedicated to moving packets. Initially called Interface Message Processors (IMPs), these devices are now known as routers, because their function is to route the packets they receive toward their destination. But the earlier name was also descriptive of another router function, which is to act as the interface between the general-purpose computer and the rest of the network. This function made it possible for router to be linked to router, so that the routers, not the general computers to which they were connected, handled all the details of communication. This was useful because it allowed Local Area Networks (LANs), the computers networked together at one location, say, an office or a building, to communicate via a single router to the larger Wide Area Network (WAN), including a WAN that provided Internet service.

In the early days of digital networks, the era of store-and-forward, each computer was addressable exclusively through a unique name or number that served as its address. To send a message, you needed to address it in much the same way as you would address the envelope of a letter, with the source address and the destination address. When computer A sent a message to computer C, computer B, the intermediate recipient, used the two addresses to pick the best route to computer C—if more than one route was available. When packet switching was added to the store-and-forward approach, not only was it necessary to have the source and destination addresses as part of each packet, but an additional piece of data was required. It was called the "offset," and it indicated the correct position of the packet in the overall message. (Remember, the packets making up a message might end up being sent out of order and even by different routes.) The offset data allows the destination computer to reassemble the packets of the message in their original order.

WHY THE INTERNET AND THE WORLD WIDE WEB ARE NOT SYNONYMS

Even more than the general-purpose computer, the router is *the* core piece of Internet hardware. Routers move packets from many sources to many destinations at the same time, all the time. Routers are the interfaces between individual computers, LANs, and WANs, on the one hand, and the Internet on the other. As the ARPANET and NSFNet developed into the Internet, an English computer scientist by the name of Tim Berners-Lee created a breakthrough that vastly expanded the very concept of digital networking by effectively liberating addresses from individual computers, at least as far as computer users were concerned. In the early 1980s, Berners-Lee worked on the now-ubiquitous concept of hypertext as a means of facilitating the sharing and updating of information among researchers on computer networks. (The hypertext concept was first articulated by the brilliant American engineer Vannevar Bush in a 1945 essay titled "As We May Think," which imagined what he called a "memex" machine capable of storing information that users could instantly access and apply whenever needed.[2] Today, hypertext is way of linking keywords in one text or dataset to related information in another text or dataset, thereby enabling a computer user to depart from a linear narrative and, with a simple mouse click, drill down into subjects related to that narrative. To put it most succinctly, hypertext enables, enhances, and facilitates information sharing over the Internet.)

Berners-Lee was employed at CERN, the Swiss-based European Organization for Nuclear Research, a global consortium of scientists who study high-energy physics.

"Well, I found it frustrating that in [the 1980s] there was different information on different computers, but you had to log on to different computers to get at it. Also, sometimes you had to learn a different program on each computer. So, finding out how things worked was really difficult. Often it was just easier to go and ask people when they were having coffee," Berners-Lee explained in a document called "Answers for Young People."[3] For Berners-Lee, digital networks and the Internet were inadequately meeting his needs; in fact, they were even failing to be at least as good as the most basic form of network: human conversation over coffee. At the same time, he realized that people connected with CERN were often not physically present at its Geneva headquarters—and so were unavailable for a coffee conversation. You cannot always personally meet everyone you want to talk to. So, he wrote some programs to convert data produced on one kind of computer using one kind of operating system to another, different computer using a different OS. The trouble was that, at the time, CERN researchers were not just using "Unix, Mac, and PC: there were all kinds of big mainframe computers and medium-sized computers running all sorts of software." Berners-Lee wanted a way not only to work with many incompatible computer and software systems spread out over a wide geographical area, but to make working with them easy, routine, and even transparent.

"Can't we convert every information system so that it looks like part of some imaginary information system which everyone can read?" he asked. "And that became the WWW"—the World Wide Web.

Today, when most of us talk about "the Internet," what we really mean is the World Wide Web. The Internet is a physical network-of-networks, a material infrastructure, whereas the WWW is a virtual "information space." The WWW is accessed via the Internet, but it is essentially a system of Uniform Resource Locators (URLs), which can be keyed to and accessed via hypertext links. This allows computer users to find and retrieve useful data with the click of a mouse.

A URL is, in effect, the address of a set of data. Computers (and other devices connected to the Internet) are identified by two numbers, a "media access control" (MAC) address and an "Internet protocol" (IP) address. The first is a kind of digital serial number hard-coded into network devices. The second is a number assigned to devices by networks that use the Internet protocol for communication. Unless you are an IT manager, engineer, or technician, you don't usually have to know either of these address numbers because you don't need them to find the data you are seeking on the Internet. True, when you want to access a certain set of data, you need to get to the computer on which it happens to reside. It's true also that the computer has a MAC address and an IP address. But all you need to know is the URL, the address of the *dataset*—not the device—you wish to access. In fact, you don't necessarily have to know even that much. As Berners-Lee explained in his "Answers for Young People," when you click on a hypertext in the document before you on your screen, you should understand that "the computer isn't showing you everything about the link. Behind the underlined or colored bit of text which you click on is an invisible thing like http://www.w3.org/. It's called a URL. This is the name of the web page to which the link goes. . . . When you click on a link, your computer takes [you to] this URL."[4]

The magic carpet most commonly used for this ride is HyperText Transfer Protocol (HTTP). In the example Berners-Lee cites, www.w3.org is the name of a particular webserver as well as its web landing page. Many hypertext links don't just take you to a server, but to a particular piece of data or document on the server. But while you, the user, are working with names that are readily understood by a human being, your computer, as Berners-Lee points out, "can't communicate with the webserver until it knows its computer number." That number is the unique Internet Protocol Address, or IP Address, assigned by a network using TCP/IP for communication. It is a series of numbers and dots that look like this, for instance: 192.168.0.1. When you click on a hyperlink, your computer must discover the IP Address before it can access the appropriate webserver and take you to the webpage with the data you want to access. To do this, your "computer makes up a packet of information," which "starts off with the number of the computer [its IP Address] the packet is going to, and then the number of the computer [its IP Address] which sent it, and then it has what the packet is about, and then whatever it is one computer is sending to the other."

Connected to the modern Internet are Domain Name System (DNS) servers. When you click a hyperlink, one of these severs retrieves the numerical IP Address associated with that hypertext. Since that the packet you sent by clicking contains the IP Address of your device, the server sends the required IP Address information to your computer, which can now access the desired webserver and webpage. The interactive communication set off by the mouse click on a hypertext link is typically routed through several computers, but because the communication is packetized, getting what you clicked on usually takes a few seconds or even less rather than the minutes or hours required by the early store-and-forward system. (Think in terms of how snail mail is delivered. You want to send a letter to John Smith who lives in the brown house on Elm Street. This is the visible portion of the hyperlink that describes the location. The postal service, however, needs something it can understand, namely 1234 Elm Street, which is the address of the location. It is the equivalent of the IP Address associated with the hyperlink, but that is not ordinarily visible to someone looking at the webpage.)

The operation of the World Wide Web can seem like magic, but it depends on two down-to-earth components: one is human coordination and cooperation, the other is physical infrastructure. Berners-Lee has modestly claimed that inventing the World Wide Web "was easy. The amazing thing which makes it work is that so many people actually have made webservers, and that they all work the same way, on the Internet. They all use HTTP." Getting them all to join in and all to "use the same sort of HTTP, and URLs, and HTML," he says, was the hard part. Today, Berners-Lee directs the World Wide Web Consortium (W3C), which coordinates the ongoing level of human cooperation needed to keep the web running.

OPENING THE BLACK BOX

As for the other part, the physical infrastructure, like the whole process of what really happens when you click on hypertext, it is largely hidden from view. When we use a desktop PC or laptop or tablet or smartphone to connect to the Internet, we sometimes talk about working or playing in "cyberspace." Actually, this term is a fiction disguising the fact that all of the individual devices and networks (LANs and WANs) connected to the Internet are physical machines. They operate as directed by a variety of software programs and are interconnected either by wires, fiber optic cable, or wireless technologies. It is all truly wonderful, a monument to the highly developed civilization of "*Homo dictyous.*" But it is also physical, complex, and vulnerable to failure caused by accident, the elements of nature, and purposeful, nefarious attack.

ACTION ITEM

The software and hardware technology of the World Wide Web hides the fact that individual networks and the Internet are *physical* infrastructures. In thinking about network security and resilience, we need to understand and appreciate that so-called cyberspace is not "space" at all, but a very substantial matrix of copper, fiber optics, semiconductors, and physical memory storage systems, all interconnected. Learn all you can about the basic structure of digital networks. This will greatly aid you in making decisions that contribute to digital resilience.

In some important respects, the basic design of the Internet includes inherently resilient elements. TCP/IP, the original "network architecture" of the Internet, demonstrates this.[5] Like any good architecture, the TCP/IP model attempts to bring together all necessary structural elements gracefully and efficiently. Also, as in any example of good architecture, durability and resilience are important qualities. The TCP/IP model consists of four "layers." From "bottom" to "top"—the bottom layer dealing with the connection between your computer and the LAN, and the top layer dealing with the interface between the networked computer and the human user—the layers are: link, internetwork, transport, and application.

Link Layer. This layer connects your computer to the LAN. The connection may be wired via Ethernet cable or may be wireless (Wi-Fi or cellular connection, depending on the device). Direct connection to a *local* area network is, indeed, local. Ethernet cable has an effective range of about a hundred meters without using a signal booster. Under ideal conditions, Wi-Fi has a maximum range of about two hundred meters.

At the link layer, two technologies—packet switching and Carrier Sense Multiple Access with Collision Detection (CSMA/CD)—exemplify the inherent resilience of the TCP/IP architecture. As discussed, breaking messages into packets avoids potentially crippling transmission delays. Packet switching is combined with CSMA/CD, by which a computer that wants to send data listens first for the presence of another computer that may already be sharing data on the network. If it hears nothing, the computer assumes the line is available, and it begins sending—while also listening for its own receive data. As long as the sending computer continues to receive its own data, it knows that it can continue to send. If the sending computer cannot receive its own data, it knows that a collision with data from another computer has occurred. In this case, both computers stop transmitting, pause, and then retry. The computers that collided wait for different lengths of time before retrying transmission. This reduces the chance of another collision. Moreover, each time a computer sends a packet of data, it pauses to allow other computers on the LAN to send. If another computer sends a packet during the pause, the first computer will wait to send its next packet until the other computer completes its packet and, in turn, pauses. Designed-in traffic control, which both reduces and resolves conflicts, is one of the resilient features of the Internet.

Internetwork Layer (IP). After a packet traverses the link layer, it has crossed the first link on its journey and is now in the router. The router looks at the destination IP Address of the packet and figures out where to send it to get it closer to its ultimate destination. The router is concerned with getting the packet over its first hop to the next computer on a plausible route to its ultimate destination. Each router at each hop looks at both destination and return IP Addresses of each packet and routes the data accordingly, always attempting to get the packet closer to its destination address.

The routers that make up the internetwork TCP/IP layer have an inherently resilient feature that recognizes traffic delays (including outages) and, when a delay is detected, signals other routers to switch to alternate routes to the destination. In this way, routers adapt to outages and other network failures on the fly.

Transport Layer (TCP). The internetwork layer, whose physical infrastructure consists of networked routers, does its best to figure out a viable path between the originating computer and the intended destination of its data packets. Despite the best efforts of the internetwork layer, however, packets sometimes get lost or significantly delayed. Often, too, the packets arrive out of order. The destination computer uses the offset data of each packet it receives to guide it in reassembling the packets into their original order.

To enhance resilience, the destination computer sends messages to the originating computer, telling it how much of the message has been received and reconstructed. If the destination computer detects missing packets, it waits and listens, assuming the packets have been delayed. After a certain period of waiting without result, the destination computer requests the originating computer to resend the errant packets.

Another resilient component of the transport layer is temporary data storage. The originating computer stores a copy of the outgoing message packets and does not delete or purge them until the destination computer acknowledges receiving the *complete* message. Key features of the transport layer are thus designed to prevent data loss.

Application Layer. The bottom three layers of the TCP/IP model are all about getting data onto the network and then moving it efficiently. The top layer, the application layer, is all about the machine-human interface, the software applications employed to make productive use of the data that has traveled from one computer to another. Familiar Internet applications include email clients and messaging and chat software. The World Wide Web itself is an Internet application, and its use is made much easier by web browsers.

Each Internet application generally consists of a *server* and a *client.* The server runs on the destination computer and listens for incoming connections over the network. Client software runs on the source computer. Email clients (such as Microsoft Outlook, Thunderbird, Apple Mail, etc.) and web browsers (Microsoft Edge, Google Chrome, Mozilla Firefox, Safari, etc.) are examples of web clients. When you interact with a website, you send data packets that are detected by the website server, which responds by (for instance) sending you a new page that features (in the case of an e-commerce website) some item of merchandise and then awaits further packets from you.

We might say that the human-machine interactive nature of the application layer is introducing an element of resilience because it enhances human oversight and control of machine interactions. On the other hand, the so-called human element is typically the most vulnerable "component" on the Internet. People make mistakes. For example, they may input data inaccurately (say, typing "legitimate" when they meant to type "illegitimate") or they may allow themselves to be duped by a fraudulent email requesting a piece of personally identifiable information (PII), such as a Social Security number. The vast majority of successful attacks on computer systems begin with "social engineering," which is a polite label for the use of fraud and deception to get into a system.

ACTION ITEM

By learning the underlying principles of digital networks, C-suite executives can communicate with technical managers and personnel more effectively. When leadership and IT professionals speak a mutually intelligible language, digital operations can be fully incorporated in the overall business plan. This promotes resilience, which is less a way of "doing" security than it is a way of doing business.

THE SURPRISING RESILIENCE OF THE INTERNET

The former U.S. National Coordinator for Security, Infrastructure Protection, and Counter-terrorism, Richard A. Clarke, is one of many security experts who have pointed to the inherent insecurity of an Internet that was originally designed for maximum openness and connectivity rather than for close control and well-locked security.[6] Clarke has a point, of course; yet I would also suggest that both the openness of the Internet and its decentralized architecture are not only essential to the network's universal utility as a tool of modern civilization, but also sources of resilience. Locking up New York City's Emergency Command Center in 7 World Trade

Center suddenly ceased to seem like a good idea on September 11, 2001, when the WTC became ground zero.[7]

Decentralization and peer-to-peer organization are not the only resilient aspects of the Internet. As we have just seen, certain aspects of TCP/IP were also designed to be resilient against failure. Nevertheless, I would concede to experts like Clarke that *security* was not high on the list of priorities among those who laid the foundation of the Internet. But decentralization and the design of TCP/IP mean that *resilience* was always a consideration. As in the many non-digital networks that coexist with the Internet—the webs spun by nature, nations, and so much else—resilience is fundamental to survival, longevity, efficiency, and utility. Resilience is not the same as security, nor is it sufficient to security. But it is *necessary* to security.

Resilience is a fundamental networking concept. Nevertheless, our digital networks remain vulnerable. The sheer volume of *successful* attacks against them is ample evidence of this. Given the extraordinary extent to which our digital and non-digital networks interact, evolving into a seamless super-network called the Internet of Things, the vulnerabilities of our digital networks are a truly existential threat. Disruption of any digital network can cascade far and wide. The "butterfly effect"—the idea that small causes can have titanic consequences—has never been more real and relevant than it is in today's intensively networked civilization.[8] And so the chapters that follow assess the impact of the Internet of Things and present strategies, policies, and tools for assessing, creating, improving, and managing digital resilience.

TAKEAWAY

Before the advent of digital technology, communication networks were black boxes. All that really mattered to business were the input and the output. The processes between these were the province of technicians, not executive managers. With the advent of digital networks, the black box approach is no longer sufficient for business leaders. CEOs and board members need to learn about the networks on which their enterprises rely. This knowledge begins with understanding the principles of digital network technology, the Internet, and the Web. In thinking about network security and resilience, we need to understand and appreciate that so-called cyberspace is not "space" at all, but a very substantial matrix of copper, fiber optics, semiconductors, and physical memory storage systems, all interconnected. C-suite leaders who learn the underlying principles of digital networks can more effectively communicate with technical managers and professional personnel. When leadership and IT professionals speak a mutually intelligible language, digital operations can be fully integrated into the overall business plan. Such integration is necessary to achieving resilience, which is less a way of "doing" security than it is a way of doing business.

5

PORTRAIT AND LANDSCAPE

Achieving Resilience in Our Fragile Digital Environment

In the Great Recession of 2007–2008, we all learned a new concept. It was called "too big to fail," and it described certain business entities—especially financial institutions—that have become so large, so interconnected, and so complex that their failure would be catastrophic to the global economic system. For this reason, governments must deem them "too big to fail" and therefore support them at any cost.

That was a debatable idea in 2007–2008. Today, it is an impossible idea, because today virtually any business can become too big to fail. Recall that the spectacularly costly cyber breach of Target (Chapter 1), a giant corporation with millions of customers, began with the *failure* of one small HVAC service contractor to avoid falling prey to a spear phishing exploit. Small as that contractor was, the connection of its compromised network to the network of Target not only compromised Target's network, but the millions of nodes beyond the network Target directly controlled, namely the credit cards of at least 40 million customers and the personally identifiable information (PII) of an additional 30 million.

We don't think of corporate behemoths as inherently fragile structures. In fact, the more connected a corporation is, the less prone to failure it seems. After all, opportunity and profit grow with connection. Yet as networks become increasingly complex, they become increasingly difficult to understand on anything approaching a granular level. The complexity and lack of understanding create instability, multiplying not only the chances of failure, but the magnitude of failure.

What, then, are the consequences of being interconnected times a trillion or more?

QUESTION: WHAT IS A TRILLION? ANSWER: INSTABILITY

Only in relatively recent times have we all become obliged to think about trillions. Consider: As of 8:10 a.m. (U.S. ET), June 6, 2017, the CBO (Congressional Budget Office), OMB (Office of Management and Budget), GOP House Committee on the Budget, and the U.S. Debt Clock can't quite agree on the amount of the national debt. They give figures ranging from more than $23 trillion (CBO) down to more than $20 trillion (GOP).[1]

Just how much is a trillion? The easy answer is 10^{12}, 10 with a dozen zeros following. But that still leaves us with a mere number. We could also try the old tricks of visualizing a trillion one-dollar bills . . .

- Stacked = 67,866 miles, or more than one-fourth the distance from the earth to the moon
- Laid as a carpet = 3,992 square miles, enough to cover an

area bigger than two Delawares

- Lined up end to end = 96,906,656 miles, greater than the distance from the earth to the sun (92.96 million miles)

If you prefer to think in temporal terms (time is money, after all), spending a trillion dollars at the rate of one dollar per second would take 31,700 years.[2]

So, multiply any of these illustrations by 20 to 23, and you might gain a (presumably horrified) notion of the magnitude of the U.S. national debt.

Or you might apply your new appreciation of "trillions" to the global digital network we call the Internet. In Chapter 2 and elsewhere, I mentioned a book by digital technology design consultants Peter Lucas, Joe Ballay, and Mickey McManus called *Trillions: Thriving in the Emerging Information Ecology*. Their subject is our "future of unbounded complexity" and how we will either profit from it as a civilization or succumb to the risks it poses. The complexity they study is a product of living and working on a network with connections in unprecedented numbers and human-machine interactions in unprecedented volume.[3]

In 2012, when the book was published, the authors were already able to report that there were "now more computers in the world than there are people. . . . In fact, there are now more computers, in the form of microprocessors, manufactured *each year* than there are living people." Most of these microprocessors do not "find their way into anything that we could recognize as a computer."[4] They are nevertheless nodes on the Internet—more specifically, on that increasingly large fraction of the Internet we call the Internet of Things (IoT). In 2012, the *Trillions* authors believed we were "arguably on the cusp of a . . . revolution: the age of Trillions" as the number of internetworked nodes reached 10^{12}. They argued that "pervasive computing" (that is, computing across nodes numbering in the trillions) "represents a profoundly different relationship of people to information" and is destined to be "understood as a distinct epoch in human history." A "decade in the era of pervasive computing," they predict, "will bring unimaginable changes." What *can* be imagined about these changes is the emergence of "instability as the status quo." Those who design and build technology will be forced to create devices increasingly dependent on context and increasingly dynamic. This, in turn, will make dynamic change standard and, therefore, bring to our pervasively networked environment an "inherent and persistent instability."[5]

INSTABILITY BECAUSE OF CHANGE IN CONTEXT

Part of the instability will come from the nature of software with functions and security parameters that change depending on the context in which they are used. Not too long ago, the standard instrumentation—what aviators call avionics—on all aircraft consisted of analog dials and toggle switches. These were the hardest of hardwired devices. Each gauge and each switch performed a specific and immutable function.

Beginning in the 1970s, however, digital (sometimes called "electronic") instrumentation was introduced, and by the end of the twentieth century, this evolved into the so-called glass cockpit, in which the hardwired dials were replaced by dynamic digital displays. They were "dynamic" in the sense that their functions changed, depending on the immediate situation—takeoff versus landing versus straight-and-level flight, for instance.

More recently, in the most advanced aircraft cockpit designs, many of the remaining toggle switches have been replaced by touchscreen controls.[6] The traditional—or at least apparent—stability of hardwired analog avionics is increasingly giving way to context-dependent, context-relevant glass cockpit digital avionics with graphical user interfaces (GUI), some of which incorporate touchscreen features.[7]

With its dynamic avionics, the glass cockpit is intended to increase what aviators call situational awareness: "appreciating all you need to know about what is going on when the full scope of your task—flying, controlling or maintaining an aircraft—is taken into account."[8] Yet the technology also introduces a certain level of that quality the *Trillions* authors call *instability*. For instance, by 2008, at least fifty glass cockpit "blackouts" had been reported on the Airbus A320, one of the most prominent among the first generation of commercial airliners to extensively employ a glass cockpit design.[9] Today, all commercial aircraft that feature a glass cockpit back up the most critical instrumentation, such as airspeed, compass, and altimeter, with traditional analog instruments.

Whether the glass cockpit enhances or diminishes situational awareness and general safety remains a subject of controversy. Some avionics experts report a negative impact on situational awareness as well as a deterioration in manual flying skills. According to a U.S. National Transportation Safety Board (NTSB) report, the glass cockpit is associated with a generally lower rate of mishaps but a higher rate of *fatal* accidents. So far, no one has offered an adequate explanation for this disconnect, but a plausible theory cites the effect of "risk homeostasis." This is a situation in which "pilots will use a safety feature to enhance the aircraft's utility rather than enjoy the increased level of safety the feature could provide. In other words, pilots use the glass cockpits to fly into conditions that they would otherwise avoid."[10]

INSTABILITY INGRAINED INTO OUR INTENSIVELY DIGITIZED ENVIRONMENT

The glass cockpit is an extreme—i.e., life-and-death—example of the kind of instability ingrained into our digital environment. The degree of instability increases as more and more digital devices become nodes on the IoT.

In the case of the glass cockpit, instability may result from such technical failures as blackout as well as the dangerous complacency created by risk homeostasis. Our civilization's increasing dependence on the Internet presents an intriguingly similar case. Instability may come from the occurrence of technical failures. For instance, "computer problems" may disrupt air travel in any number of ways: air traffic control equipment may fail, airline reservation systems may fail, Immigration Customs and Enforcement (ICE) systems may fail.[11] Instability may also result from risk homeostasis. It is this phenomenon that makes phishing exploits successful, as email users, accustomed to clicking on links in official-looking messages, do so confidently and even reflexively. Digital fraud contributes significantly to instability in our digitally connected world. Indeed, it is reasonable to attribute the potentially destabilizing effect of fake news and hoaxes on risk homeostasis created by widespread unquestioning acceptance of information conveyed via the Internet.

ACTION ITEM

Know the limits of your network's security measures. Avoid the dangerous complacency of assuming that firewalls and antimalware software will not only defeat all attacks, but will do so without human intervention and judgment. Almost all

> cyberattacks that succeed do so because of human error. A computer user, accustomed to clicking on links in myriad email messages sent by familiar companies, readily becomes complacent. Failing to recognize any risk in reflexively clicking on what appears to be a bona-fide link in a bona-fide email, he clicks, unwittingly admitting a Trojan or ransomware or other malware into the network. Knowledge, awareness, and judgment—all human attainments—are critically necessary components of a resilient machine-human network. Digital automation *engenders* complacency but *requires* heightened vigilance and the exercise of informed judgment.

HOW THE WORLD WIDE WEB CREATES INSTABILITY

Other factors contribute to digitally induced instability. First, there is the sheer volume of data circulating, flowing, and surging over the global Internet. Quite apart from instability nefariously created by cybercriminals, who compromise data and steal identities, intellectual property, state secrets, or money, or who crash networks by means of distributed denial of service (DDoS) attacks, a key feature of the World Wide Web destabilizes our access to data.

Let me explain.

Anyone who went to college before the ascendency of the Internet remembers reading and writing innumerable research papers that included a bibliography. The word *bibliography* strongly smells of the pre-online era. Derived from Greek via Latin, *bibliography* literally means "book writing," and a bibliography is essentially a list of books, typically books the author of a scholarly essay acknowledges as the sources of the essay. Reading a paper essay with a paper bibliography even years after it was written, one can be reasonably certain of locating all of the bibliographical sources in some library somewhere or, perhaps, some combination of libraries. Today, however, a bibliography is more than "book writing." Typically, any number of online sources are included. Often, the Internet is the only platform on which the sources are readily available, and the World Wide Web is the only practical means of accessing them. This can be a very great convenience, of course, both for the writer of a scholarly work and for readers who want to consult the listed sources. All you need do is click on a hyperlink in the bibliography (or perhaps in the body of the text) or copy and paste a URL.

But who of us hasn't had the experience of working with an "old" online document—that is, a document perhaps ten, maybe five, maybe just two years old; maybe even a few months or weeks old—and clicking, in vain, on a dead link? "Fifty years from now, what percentage of [today's] web references will still be operational?" the authors of *Trillions* ask. "We will be very surprised if the answer turns out to be greater than zero."[12]

In Chapter 4, we discussed the creation of the URL—the Uniform Resource Locator—as a great advance for the human-digital network interface. True enough, for it made the World Wide Web a practical possibility. Without the URL, even if your computer were plugged into the global network, you would need to know the numerical IP address of a computer or server on which the data you seek is stored. The URL translates the machine-friendly series of numbers into a human-friendly letter- or word-based pointer to a data location on a computer network and serves as a mechanism for retrieving the sought-after data.

When you click on a hyperlink or type in a URL, you are accessing a node on the Internet. Functionally, however, the clicking *feels* as if you are directly accessing the one piece of data or the one dataset you want. This is *way* better than the old-fashioned printed library catalog card, which gave you the author and title of the book you wanted, together with its Library of Congress Control Number (LCCN) or (in some libraries) its Dewey Decimal Classification number, then sent you on your way to retrieve the book on the library shelf. Of course, that took some legwork, and then, even with book in hand, you often had to find the single page—perhaps even the single sentence—you wanted. This is nowhere near as quick and easy and efficient as clicking on a hyperlink, which will take you not just to the "book" or even to the sentence, but right down to the very *word* you seek.

Unless the link is dead. Then you will go nowhere and find nothing.

In the pre-digital library, it was always possible that the book listed in the card file was not on the shelf at that moment. The library's copy or copies might all be in the hands of others, or someone might have mis-shelved the item. Nevertheless, because most books were printed in at least comparatively large numbers—and many in truly massive numbers—you could be quite confident that you would find the volume you sought somewhere. It might be inconvenient or difficult to find, or the library's particular copy might be missing, but the data was almost certainly not lost forever.

This is not always the case with a dead link or a URL that is no longer functioning. "If you quote from and cite, say, *Moby-Dick,* everyone understands that you are not referencing one particular instance of that book. Any of the millions upon millions of more or less identical replicas of Melville's words will (for most purposes) do equally well." In contrast, the URL you cite does not point "to a web page that has been massively replicated like a published book." It is a unique address that "will remain relevant only as long as the owner of that 'place' [on the World Wide Web] possesses the resources and the will to maintain the pointer." How long will that be? No one knows, but we can safely assume it will be far from forever. "Sooner or later, all links on the World Wide Web will go dead."[13]

The *Trillions* authors quite reasonably judge that this degree of instability is "no way to run a civilization." Yet we all blithely cling to URLs as "the primary way that knowledge workers around the world document their thinking and research," even though these pointers generally have "a half-life of only a few years" at most.[14] When a data item or dataset loses all connection with an operational URL, it becomes inaccessible. This may not be as kinetically dramatic an instance of wanton data destruction as the burning of the Library of Alexandria or Henry VIII's sacking of the monasteries (Chapter 3), but when data becomes inaccessible it is effectively lost just the same. Relying on URLs to protect data—"protect" in the sense of preserving the accessibility of the information—is about as resilient a network strategy as building your house on sand.

CLOUDY WITH A CHANCE OF INSTABILITY

But let us for the moment hold in abeyance further discussion of the alarming instability of the URL-based World Wide Web and turn to today's most popular digital strategy for data protection: cloud data storage or cloud data backup.

Begin with the very image of a "cloud." In the context of data backup, storage, and retrieval, *cloud* is like *cyberspace* as it is used to describe the Internet. That is, both words are fictions. More than that, both are *dangerous* fictions, because they obscure rather than reveal and express the nature of the things they describe. Both terms evoke something ethereal, heavenly, or celestial. They connote the eternal. Best to stick a pin in this hyperinflated delusion.

Lately, I keep hearing sensible people saying "the cloud is just someone else's computer." The fuller truth is that the underlying nature of both "cyberspace" and "the cloud" is intensively and pervasively physical. Both rely on machines, cables, connections, satellites, transmitters, and receivers. Like all physical systems, such things are far from eternal, but, on the contrary, vulnerable to mechanical failure and breakdown, as well as to nefarious tampering. They are also costly. They are owned, operated, maintained, and controlled, for the most part, by corporate entities with profit motives.

While capitalism may long endure, no corporation is forever. True, some companies have lasted a very long time. For instance, in Japan, more than 20,000 firms are more than a hundred years old, and a few are more than a thousand years old. Nishiyama Onsen Keiunkan, a hotel located in Hayakawa, Yamanashi Prefecture, in the Japanese Alps, has been operating continuously since AD 705, making it the oldest company in the world.[15] But the more than 20,000 hundred-year-old-plus companies in Japan, together with the handful that exceed a thousand years, are extreme outliers in global business. "The average lifespan of a company listed in the S&P 500 index of leading U.S. companies has decreased by more than fifty years in the last century, from sixty-seven years in the 1920s to just fifteen years today," according to Professor Richard Foster from Yale University. Foster says that today's "rate of change 'is at a faster pace than ever,'" and "he estimates that by 2020, more than three-quarters of the S&P 500 will be companies that we have not heard of yet."[16]

The average lifespan of a Fortune 500 (or equivalent) multinational corporation is forty to fifty years. A third of companies listed in the 1970 Fortune 500 were gone by 1983.[17] In other words, the life expectancy of our biggest, most established corporations is little more than half the average lifespan of a human being. And yet it is such corporate entities—or lesser ones—that own the so-called cloud. The "bottom line," say the authors of *Trillions,* "is that as long as you choose to trust all of your data to a single commercial entity, those data will remain available to you no longer than the lifetime of that entity and its successors."[18] Blanche Dubois, the impecunious and insecure aging Southern belle of Tennessee Williams's *A Streetcar Named Desire,* "always relied on the kindness of strangers." We grasp an even thinner reed when we rely on strangers whose stewardship of our data ends when they cease to turn a profit.

AS A DIGITAL CIVILIZATION, WE CLING TO INSTABILITY

At the heart of digital resilience is the imperative to protect data. Yet, as a digital civilization, we cling to a highly unstable URL tool for identifying, locating, and retrieving data on our global network, and we rely on profit-driven private-sector corporations to safeguard our most critical data. Industry associations, governments, and global institutions need to create some resilient alternatives to this inherently unstable data infrastructure. It is a matter critical to civilization. If the Library of Alexandria can be burned, a corporate cloud can be switched off. Same devastating effect.

Some have suggested that we return to the essence of the Internet as it was originally conceived in 1969, as a true peer-to-peer (P2P) network, owned by everyone and by no one. In this model, networking is radically distributed and its resilience derives from the very absence of central control. The *Trillions* authors believe that the architecture of such a network could be designed such that "every time a node appears or disappears, the network automatically reconfigures, and, of course, if properly designed, it scales forever." Because there is no single central repository, it is a "real cloud," which means that the network can "withstand attackers," and because it is not owned, "it can't be shot down by its own proprietors either."[19] Such a radically distributed architecture could make possible a "true Information Commons," in which data would not be stored on one or a handful of servers, but would be massively replicated (like those copies of *Moby-Dick*) on many computer systems accessible peer-to-peer.[20] Instead of relying on inherently ephemeral URLs to access data, each unit of data that is intended to be universally available will be entered into the Commons and assigned a "universally unique identifier,"[21] unambiguous, readily searchable, and as close to eternal as anything human can be.

ACTION ITEM

Recognize that our individual networks, no matter how resilient we may work to make them, are connected to an inherently unstable—and therefore insufficiently resilient—Internet. The URLs we use to access data are impermanent, even ephemeral. The cloud storage, although handy for both accessibility and security, is a network, subject to the same insecurities and instabilities that threaten all networks and subject to the whims of profit-driven operation and ownership. Consider becoming an activist in the promotion of a more resilient Internet infrastructure and a data accessibility solution more durable and resilient than the URL. In the meantime, take proactive steps to ensure the security and permanence of your data storage. Do not take the permanence of "the cloud" for granted.

Of course, the "Commons" alternative to corporately owned clouds and papier-mâché URLs is not a plan. It is at best a call for a plan. But it is hardly without precedent, which is none other than the Internet as originally conceived, the Internet that likewise began life as a call for a plan. If it still seems "visionary"—as in very nice but not very practical—we must ask ourselves just how "practical" it is to continue to put all our precious digital eggs in a basket that is shallow, ragged, and full of holes, a basket that becomes less and less resilient the more we heap into it.

THE PHYSICAL INSTABILITY OF THE INTERNET

Although massively distributing publicly accessible data on a true P2P network would increase the resilience of the Internet, it can never transform the Internet into a true realm of cyber*space,* an ethereal region in which information somehow floats free. The necessity of a physical infrastructure will always give the lie to the *space* half of "cyberspace," because the reality is that "cyberspace" has what IT experts call a "backbone." This is the trunk line of the Internet.

There are hundreds of Internet service providers (ISPs) in the United States, but only a handful of so-called Tier 1 ISPs that control the backbone that, in turn, connects directly with the smaller ISPs. The U.S. "Tier 1 Club" includes AT&T, Verizon, Sprint, Century Link, Level 3, NTT/Verio, and Cogent. The backbone they own or control consists of hundreds of thousands of miles of fiber optic cable bundles. The overland portion of this backbone network connects at the shoreline to undersea fiber optic cables. As we know, the Internet is massive and complex, a many-branching network. Yet its backbone is relatively simple—and quite vulnerable to both digital and physical attack. If an attacker wishes to take down or to otherwise compromise the Internet, there is no portion of the global network that provides an attacker greater leverage, yields more bang for the buck, than the backbone. As reported in a 2015 article in the *MIT Technology Review*, "It is disturbingly easy to attack the backbone of the Internet to block access to a major online service like YouTube, or to intercept online communications on a vast scale."[22]

Security researchers point to "longstanding weaknesses in the protocol that works out how to route data across the different networks making up the Internet. Almost all the infrastructure running that protocol does not even use a basic security technology that would make it much harder to block or intercept data." This technology is available, but it is not being used, presumably (as Wim Remes of the security company Rapid7 explains) because there is "limited probability of these attacks"; however, he points out, "the impact once they happen is huge."[23]

The significant weakness is in the border gateway protocol (BGP), which is employed by the large routers of the Tier 1 ISPs (among others) "to figure out how to get data [from the backbone] to different places." BGP lacks "security mechanisms . . . to verify the information they are receiving or the identity of the routers providing it."[24] This is a deficiency that has been known for decades and was "the basis of the hacking group L0pht's 1998 claim before Congress that they could take down the Internet in thirty minutes." Indeed, a hitherto unexplained 2008 diversion of U.S. web traffic via Belarus and Iceland may have been the result of an attack on routers at the backbone.[25] The security company Qrator Labs has also demonstrated that "BGP could be manipulated to obtain a security certificate in the name of a particular website without permission, making it possible to impersonate [the website] and decrypt secured traffic."[26]

Because the Internet is widely distributed, attacks at one or even many nodes may have significant, possibly dire, consequences, but they are unlikely to bring the whole network down. The closer a hacker gets to the backbone, however, the greater the consequences of a massively successful attack. Among the prime targets for anyone bent on global disruption are the undersea cables, fiber optic bundles that carry 99 percent of all transoceanic digital communication.

On October 25, 2015, Pentagon officials reported concern that Russian submarines and "spy ships" were "aggressively operating near the vital undersea cables." This raised "concerns among some American military and intelligence officials that the Russians might be planning to attack those lines in times of tension or conflict."[27] The crudest kind of attack would use a submarine to place and detonate an explosive charge near a cable to blast it apart and sever it.

The Russians have already employed disruptive attacks against the Internet during times of political tension and war. In 2007, Russian-based hackers mounted three weeks of massive distributed denial of service attacks against Estonia after "a row that erupted . . . over the Estonians' removal of the Bronze Soldier Soviet war memorial in central Tallinn." The "websites of government ministries, political parties, newspapers, banks, and companies" were disrupted.[28] To this day, there is no conclusive proof directly connecting the Russian government to the cyberattacks, but circumstantial evidence abounds. Konstantin Goloskokov, a leading member of a pro-Kremlin Russian youth organization called Nashi, admitted that Nashi had been involved. Goloskokov was not only a Nashi activist, he was also assistant to Sergei Markov, a Duma Deputy (the equivalent of a U.S. member of Congress).

A Russian word meaning "ours," Nashi is the short form of "Youth Democratic Anti-Fascist Movement 'NASHI.'" The organization is officially funded by *private* Russian business interests, but its creation on April 15, 2005, was enthusiastically endorsed by the Russian government. And, by 2007, Nashi was receiving the vigorous endorsement of prominent government figures, including Vladislav Surkov, who was then first deputy chief of the presidential staff and subsequently Russia's deputy prime minister.[29] In 2008, Russia invaded the Republic of Georgia (which had become independent from the Soviet Union in 1991) in a successful effort to break off two self-proclaimed republics, South Ossetia and Abkhazia, from Georgia and establish a Russian military presence in them. The invasion and "kinetic" battle were preceded by Russian cyberwarfare attacks.[30]

As for cable sabotage, it is nothing new and "was common during both World Wars." During the Cold War, the Soviets were suspected of tampering with the transatlantic cable off Newfoundland, and the U.S. Navy deployed divers from submarines to tap into Soviet military communication in Operation Ivy Bells. But even non-nefarious activities are a menace to transoceanic cable. Such things as "dropped anchors and fishing nets" account for "about 60 percent of cut cable incidents."[31]

Operation Ivy Bells, which began in the 1970s, ended abruptly in 1981 when an NSA employee, Ronald Pelton, sold Ivy Bells information to the Soviets for $35,000.[32] The betrayal of Ivy Bells did not permanently end tapping of the undersea portion of the Internet's backbone, however. As revealed by NSA contractor Edward Snowden through material he leaked via WikiLeaks and interviews published in *The Guardian, Washington Post, Der Spiegel,* and *The New York Times,* the U.K. GCHQ (Government Communications Headquarters) and the U.S. NSA operated collaboratively to tap virtually all digital data traveling through undersea cables. The volume was tremendous. Just one British program, Tempora, was vacuuming up some 21 million gigabytes every day. Snowden's revelations concerning the NSA PRISM/US-984XN program exposed a technologically advanced operation for analyzing the raw data acquired through eavesdropping on the cable traffic.[33]

The actual tapping of the undersea cables, however, is strictly old-school, "extremely secretive, but . . . similar to tapping an old-fashioned, pre-digital telephone line" at locations along some 550,000 miles of cable about the diameter of a garden hose.[34] A 2005 Associated Press report published in *The New York Times* and elsewhere described the USS *Jimmy Carter* (SSN-23), a nuclear submarine commissioned in February 2005 and fitted out with "a special capability . . . to tap undersea cables," presumably by deploying Navy SEALs or other specialized divers to "physically place . . . tap[s] . . . along the [cable] route."[35] The locations most vulnerable to physical taps are at "regeneration points," where devices amplify signals at intervals in what is a very long journey. "At these spots, the fiber optics can be more easily tapped, because they are no longer bundled together, rather laid out individually."[36]

Of course, physically tapping cables would be easier to do on dry land than underwater, but this is impossible if the undersea cable makes landfall on the coastline of an unfriendly or unwilling country. Fortunately for the NSA, the U.K. is both friendly and willing, and, because of its Atlantic island location, it is the terminus of many cable routes. Tappers use so-called intercept probes to make the physical taps. These "small devices . . . capture the light being sent across the [fiber optic] cable. The probe bounces the light through a prism, makes a copy of it, and turns it into binary data without disrupting the flow of the original Internet traffic."[37]

THE INSTABILITY OF THE HUMAN-MACHINE INTERFACE

The physical infrastructure of the global Internet is massively vulnerable from a security point of view, even in mid-ocean or where ocean meets land. The most numerous network weak spots, however, are the millions, billions, and, yes, trillions of nodes on the global Internet. The places where devices—ranging from desktop, laptop, and tablet computers to smart thermostats to smart valve control devices on oil and natural gas pipelines to smart televisions to personal performance and health devices (such as smart watches)—communicate with digital networks are the entry-exit ports of the Internet. Physical taps are possible at many of these nodes, but they are hardly necessary for eavesdropping. As we saw in the case of the Target breach (Chapter 1), malware programs conveyed by the Internet itself are the most effective means of infiltrating targeted networks and computers. In some cases, the malware is installed purposely by someone onsite—a rogue employee, perhaps, or a covert agent armed with a program on a USB thumb drive. Most of the time, however, the malware is installed remotely by means of "social engineering" confidence tricks that include:

- Pretexting—in which the attacker invents a scenario that deceives an innocent insider into doing or divulging something that gains the attacker access to the targeted network or computer.
- Theft by diversion—in which the attacker persuades an innocent insider to divert data or messages intended for a legitimate recipient to a different target.
- Phishing—the most common means of attack, which typically uses an email that appears to come from a legitimate source (often a bank, credit card company, or business)

requesting "verification" of personally identifiable information (PII) to avert some serious and unwanted consequence (usually suspension of an account). Skilled attackers create counterfeit emails that are virtually identical, logo graphics and all, to legitimate emails the company might send. Attackers also tend to counterfeit messages from firms with immense customer bases, so that the chance of the email being read by an actual customer is quite high.

- Spear fishing—a specialized form of phishing, in which the attacker obtains certain specific information on the target and uses it to customize a counterfeit email. If the information is accurate, the customization greatly increases the odds of the attack succeeding. The 2016 hack of the Democratic National Committee (see Chapter 3) was an instance of spear phishing targeted against a high-level campaign official, Hillary Clinton campaign chairman John Podesta.
- Phone phishing—another phishing subset also sometimes known as IVR phishing. Using an automated interactive voice response (IVR) device, the attacker simulates a call from a legitimate business (typically a bank or credit card company), prompting the callee to "verify" account and identity information (especially PIN numbers and passwords) by entering them via the telephone touchpad. The verification is urgently requested to avoid account suspension.

Collectively, these social engineering attacks employ age-old confidence tricks adapted to digital technology. Moreover, many phishing exploits, including some of the most common and destructive, require very little crafty persuasion. They simply prey on our natural curiosity or greed. Emails are blasted to tens or hundreds of thousands of addressees, inviting the recipient to click on a link to obtain something *free* or at an impossibly steep discount, or to see something *interesting* or *new*. The recipient who yields to curiosity and clicks the link inadvertently opens an executable file that installs a malware program, which infiltrates and compromises the local network on which the computer is located.

Because such exploits are so common, many computer users have become sufficiently savvy to avoid clicking on links found in unsolicited emails from unknown senders. No matter. Many malware programs introduced via executable email attachments hijack the user's email account, using it to send the attacker's emails—just as if they were being sent from the hijacked user's account. Moreover, in hijacking the email account, the malware also accesses the targeted user's address book or contact list, so that the counterfeit emails are sent not only from the targeted user's address but to recipients who know and presumably trust the targeted user. People too levelheaded to open an attachment associated with an unsolicited email from a stranger often open, without a second thought, an attachment apparently sent from a known and trusted source.

ACTION ITEM

Understand that malware is often used to infiltrate and hijack email accounts, thereby giving spammers and other cyber fraudsters the ability to send phishing emails to everyone in the address book of the infiltrated email account holder. To the recipient, these fraudulent emails appear to come from someone they know. Even spear phishing emails sent from the email account of a friend or colleague are usually fairly easy to spot. Do not click on any attachment in an email from a known sender if the content of the email seems uncharacteristic of the sender. For example, a vendor with whom you have a business relationship is unlikely to send an email that begins "Now is your chance to get that job you really want. . . ." If the content of an email is doubtful, contact the sender to ask about it. You can reduce the likelihood that your own email account will be hijacked by periodically changing your account password.

Network attacks based on social engineering demonstrate that the most vulnerable network nodes—or, more accurately, the most vulnerable components of a given network node—are human. The softest target is the person behind the screen and with a finger on the mouse or a pair of thumbs on the virtual keyboard of a smartphone or who, suffering password overload, fails to create a password or change the default password when he or she sets up a new smart thermostat or other device on the IoT. We ourselves are the weakest link in our digital networks. We ourselves are the reason the hardware and software of our networks must be made resilient. Of course, we human beings are educable. But will we heed the lessons? Yes. But do we make mistakes? Sure.

INSTABILITY ON THE INTERNET OF THINGS

Whether they are in business for themselves, employed by organized crime, employed by "legitimate" companies, or employed by governments (as civilians, freelancers, or members of the military), hackers are not waiting to find out the answers to these questions. As noted in Chapter 2, in October 2016, Dyn, an Internet performance management company whose products control much of the DNS, the Internet's vital domain name system, came under two massive distributed denial of service (DDoS) attacks.

DDoS attacks are common, but what made these 2016 attacks newsworthy was that they used the Mirai botnet to infect a very large number of computers, forcing an attack that overwhelmed Dyn servers. As *The Guardian* reported, "Unlike other botnets, which are typically made up of computers, the Mirai botnet is largely made up of [far more numerous and less well defended] . . . 'internet of things' (IoT) devices."[38] Shortly after the Mirai botnet attacks were revealed, Senator Mark Warner (D-Va.) called for "improved tools to better protect American consumers, manufacturers, retailers, Internet sites and service providers," and Mark Dufresne, director of threat research at Endgame, a Virginia-based cybersecurity company, warned of "the dangers of this IoT running rampant," aided and abetted by "bad to middling security [with] nobody . . . knocking it out of the park."[39]

Although exploiting the IoT with botnets is a new wrinkle in mounting DDoS attacks, security concerns over the interface between computer software and devices in the "real world" have been around for a long time and actually predate the rise of the Internet. Back in January 1982, "President Ronald Reagan approved a CIA plan to sabotage the economy of the Soviet Union through covert transfers of technology that contained hidden malfunctions," including software with embedded features—called "logic bombs"—designed to trigger catastrophic equipment failures. When a KGB insider revealed to U.S. government agents that the Soviets were looking to steal advanced SCADA (Supervisory Control And Data Acquisition) software for running natural gas pipeline control apparatus (pumps, turbines, and valves), the CIA persuaded a Canadian firm that designed such software to insert a logic bomb into a program the agency knew the KGB would steal. As Thomas C. Reed, former U.S. Secretary of the Air Force and Reagan administration Director of the National Reconnaissance Office, recounted in his 2004 memoir, *At the Abyss: An Insider's History of the Cold War*, the purloined software was duly installed to control critical machinery along Soviet natural gas pipelines. After what Reed called "a decent interval," the embedded logic bomb caused a reset of "pump speeds and valve settings to produce pressures far beyond those acceptable to pipeline joints and welds. The result was the most monumental non-nuclear explosion and fire ever seen from space." Reed reported that "there were no physical casualties from the pipeline explosion," but "there was significant damage to the Soviet economy."[40]

The Russians proved themselves remarkably adept at using digital means to tamper with real-world events during the 2007 dispute with Estonia over its removal of "the Bronze Soldier of Tallinn" from a downtown city park to the Defense Forces Cemetery outside of the capital city proper. By 2007, Estonia had earned the sobriquet "e-Stonia" because it was perhaps the most thoroughly wired nation in Europe. Its 1.3 million people were intensively networked. By November 2005, the government had shifted most of its operations entirely to the Internet. All official documents were executed and signed electronically. Cabinet-level meetings were conducted in cyberspace, and Estonians voted entirely online. In 2007, 61 percent of the Estonian population accessed their bank accounts online—exclusively—and, overall, 95 percent of all banking transactions were electronic.[41]

While ethnic Russians living in Tallinn staged protests against the removal of the Bronze Soldier, the nation was barraged by DDoS attacks, in which botnets consisting of tens of thousands of computers overwhelmed key Estonian websites with log-on requests, thereby disabling them. The botnets were international, networked systems normally used by disreputable e-commerce providers to disseminate spam. During these attacks, Russian online chat rooms buzzed with calls to action and included instructions on how to participate in the DDoS attacks. Estonian "government websites that normally receive 1,000 visits a day reportedly were receiving 2,000 visits every second." The servers of a government network designed to handle 2 million megabits of traffic per second were flooded with some 200 million megabits per second. In one ten-hour-plus sustained attack, more than 90 million megabits per second of data were unleashed against Estonian targets. These included the websites of the Ministries of Foreign Affairs and Justice, which were beaten into a total shutdown. The Reform Party website was defaced with digital graffiti that included a cookie-duster mustache scrawled, à la Hitler, across the face of Prime Minister Andrus Ansip. And then, on May 3, the botnets turned DDoS attacks against Estonian private-sector websites and servers. This quickly forced most of the country's banks to shut down, the ripples of the attack reaching well into the international banking community.[42]

Moscow vigorously denied involvement in the attacks, the volume of which peaked on May 9, 2007, the Russian anniversary of the end of World War II. More recently, of course, Russia attacked the 2015–2016 U.S. presidential campaign and election. In a statement eerily reminiscent of the 2007 cyberattacks on Estonia, Russian President Vladimir Putin told reporters at the St. Petersburg Economic Forum that "'patriotic hackers' may have meddled in the U.S. election, but insisted that none of their potential activities were state-backed." He even likened these individuals to "'artists,' who could act on behalf of Russia if they felt its interests were being threatened." Artists, Putin said, "may act on behalf of their country, they wake up in good mood and paint things. Same with hackers, they woke up today, read something about the state-to-state relations. If they are patriotic, they contribute in a way they think is right, to fight against those who say bad things about Russia."[43] Yet the Russian president denied that his government had launched the attacks.

By the peak of the 2007 attacks on Estonia, the Estonian government managed to respond to the onslaught by quadrupling the data capacity of its systems, and the attacks began to subside. On May 15, however, Russian hacktivists did manage, albeit briefly, to disable the national toll-free emergency phone number. In 2004, Estonia had joined NATO, which responded to the 2007 DDoS attacks by looking into the possibility of invoking Article 5 of the NATO charter, a provision that obligates all members to respond to an act of war against any member as an act of aggression against itself. NATO quickly backed down, however, because, as the Estonian minister of defense explained, "At present, NATO does not define cyberattacks as a clear military action. This means that the provisions of Article 5 of the North Atlantic Treaty . . . will not automatically be extended to the attacked country."

Commenting on NATO's dithering, one historian observed, "Technology had transformed NATO's ring of steel around its members to a fence of tissue paper."[44] The attack did, however, move NATO to create the Cooperative Cyber Defense Centre of Excellence (CCDCOE) in Tallinn beginning in 2008. Eight years later, it should be observed, in 2016, retired Admiral James Stavridis, who commanded NATO from 2009 to 2013, cited the DNC hacks in his assessment of the current state of U.S. digital networks. "It is the greatest mismatch between the level of threat, very high, and the level of preparation, quite low," he said on December 15, 2016. "We're headed toward a cyber Pearl Harbor, and it is going to come at either the grid or the financial sector."[45]

CREATING DIGITAL RESILIENCE ONE NODE AT A TIME

In its early evolution from the ARPANET and NSFNet, the Internet incorporated in its architecture and protocols the rudiments of resilience (Chapter 4). As the Internet has grown from four networked university computer systems (at UCLA, Stanford, UC Santa Barbara, and the University of Utah) in 1969 to quite probably a trillion or more nodes in 2016, it has become less rather than more resilient. Senator Warner has called for "improved tools to better protect American consumers, manufacturers, retailers, Internet sites and service providers." This is laudable, but we need more than tools. We need—and by *we*, I mean all stakeholders in the Internet, which is very nearly everyone on our intensively networked planet—to create a culture that prioritizes resilience. To be sure, we must give security a high priority, but we also must acknowledge that no practical degree of security will ever be bulletproof.

We need to design our systems to withstand the inevitable shots that manage to find their targets. In the meantime, we must recognize that the Internet is vulnerable, which means that our thoroughly intertwined digital and analog networks—physical, social, political, financial, mechanical, and kinetic—have created an inherently unstable, insecure, and nonresilient environment. This being the case, we must design whatever networks we control to be resilient. Whether those networks consist of a handful of devices connected to the Internet or a vast corporate intranet that connects thousands of nodes to the Internet, we must take measures to ensure their resilience. This is a matter of immediate self-defense and the defense of those who are our customers, employees, and investors. This is also our contribution to the defense of the Internet we all share. Each resilient node and element of resilient architecture we add to the Internet contributes to our collective digital resilience.

TAKEAWAY

In an intensively interconnected world, instability is the status quo. We rely heavily on digitally networked devices with functions and security parameters that change depending on the context in which they are used. Because these dynamic changes are automated, we remain largely unaware of the underlying instability. Indeed, digital automation *engenders* complacency but actually *requires* heightened vigilance and the thoughtful exercise of informed judgment. We must act both individually and collaboratively—as members of a digital society and civilization—to increase the resilience of the networks we control directly as well as those to which we connect.

6

THE MEASURE OF RESILIENCE

Assessing and Improving Your Digital Resilience

Back in high school, I read Herman Melville's *Moby-Dick,* one of those datasets formerly known as a book, reproduced in the millions and therefore in little danger of disappearing when some unique URL goes dead. Aside from Ahab and the Whale, one episode has stuck with me through the years, and I know why. It's about networks. I recently reread it.

It's Chapter 72, "The Monkey-Rope," and it describes a bit of whaler's gear called by that name. Ishmael (the novel's protagonist and narrator) ties one end of the monkey-rope around his waist and stands on deck while the "harpooneer," Queequeg, ties the other end around his waist and is lowered down on the half-submerged harpooned whale tied up alongside the ship. Queequeg's task is to plant a "blubber-hook" into the dead animal, so that it can be cut into transportable pieces that are loaded aboard ship. The sea is rough (in the language of network analysis, it is "unstable"), and hungry sharks, drawn by blood in the water, circle round and round. Queequeg's life depends on Ishmael, and Ishmael's on Queequeg. If Ishmael lets Queequeg slip, the harpooneer could be crushed between the whale carcass and the ship's hull or he could become instant shark food. If Queequeg should fall, he would likely pull Ishmael down with him. "So strongly and metaphysically did I conceive of my situation then," Ishmael tells us, "that while earnestly watching his [Queequeg's] motions, I seemed distinctly to perceive that my own individuality was now merged in a joint stock company of two; . . . that another's mistake or misfortune might plunge innocent me into unmerited disaster and death. . . ." This situation seemed to Ishmael "a gross . . . injustice" aimed squarely at himself.

> And yet still further pondering—while I jerked [Queequeg] now and then from between the whale and ship, which would threaten to jam him—still further pondering, I say, I saw that this situation of mine was the precise situation of every mortal that breathes; only, in most cases, he, one way or other, has this Siamese connexion with a plurality of other mortals. If your banker breaks, you snap; if your apothecary by mistake sends you poison in your pills, you die. True, you may say that, by exceeding caution, you may possibly escape these and the multitudinous other evil chances of life. But handle Queequeg's monkey-rope heedfully as I would, sometimes he jerked it so, that I came very near sliding overboard. Nor could I possibly forget that, do what I would, I only had the management of one end of it.[1]

For Melville and his Ishmael, the monkey-rope is a metaphor of the essential interconnectedness of life in a civilized society. You may imagine you are independent and entirely self-determined, responsible for your debts and signature only, as the legal phrase goes, but no man is an island and do not ask for whom the bell tolls. In my own metaphysical mood, I see Melville's monkey-rope as a metaphor of the even more intensively interconnected condition of today's digital networks. You may imagine that your VPN, your firewalls, your lengthy passwords, your antimalware software, and your rigorously observed safe-computing practices make you independent and entirely self-determined. Let's even say that yours is so small a business that you personally know and can vouch for every single person on your company LAN.

What could possibly go wrong?

Assuming your modest little cul-de-sac is connected to the Internet, possibly anything, possibly everything. You and your company are tied by the waist to the whole wired-in world. It is a world, as Chapter 5 suggests, that is far more complex than anything Herman Melville could have envisioned in 1851. Ishmael and Queequeg were tied together, one to one. But each of us is tied to potentially trillions of network nodes and, through them, to millions, even billions, of people. How do we even begin to get a handle on such a network?

THE END OF SECURITY—AND WHAT TO DO ABOUT IT

When computers were widely introduced to government and business during the 1960s—it was the era of "big iron," the age of the mainframe—the principal security issue was physical security. Computer facilities had raised floors, special air conditioning, and were carefully secured from onsite tampering with keycard locks accessible by "authorized" people only. When people and businesses first went online (but not yet on the Internet) in a big way during the early 1980s, a period that coincided with rise of the "personal computer" and the gradual retreat of the mainframe, cybersecurity rapidly emerged as an issue. Initially, the problem was "hackers" uploading malware of various sorts mostly via floppy disk. So, yet again, security was largely an onsite issue. But as local area and wide area networks (LANs and WANs) began to play an increasingly important part in the way businesses and other institutions used computers—and then with the emergence of the Internet in earnest in the mid-1990s—the concern became specifically online security. Malware could be uploaded remotely and systems thereby compromised.

This era saw the proliferation of viruses and, correspondingly, antivirus software as well as such network security systems as hardware and software firewalls. Such "point solutions" worked reasonably well against "point threats," which were mostly virus-based attacks that were well understood. Because the early viruses had identifiable "signatures," they were relatively easy to identify and neutralize. For years, a host of antivirus companies diligently collected the latest viruses, quickly developed appropriate antivirus modules, and promptly distributed updates ("patches") to their installed antivirus products. Provided that users kept their security software patched and therefore up to date, they were reasonably secure against most threats.

ACTION ITEM

Application vulnerabilities are continually discovered, and attackers ceaselessly develop new malware. Software patching, therefore, remains essential to cybersecurity. Most of the updates software makers supply on a regular basis are related to patching newly discovered vulnerabilities, meeting new malware threats, or generally improving security. Do not fail to install updates and patches as they are received. Most of the larger software makers offer push or even automatic updates. Enable these. IT managers need to ensure that all devices on their networks are routinely updated and patched. Threats are dynamic. Defending against them must be dynamic as well.

The era of cybersecurity based solely or primarily on antivirus, antimalware, and firewall solutions is over. Don't get me wrong. These point solutions to point threats are still very necessary, in fact, essential to good cybersecurity practices, but they are no longer sufficient to it. Not by a long shot. Today's cyber threats are commensurate with today's trillion-node Internet. They are, in a word, overwhelming—overwhelming in terms of their complexity as well as in their sheer volume. The threats come from everywhere. They are inside, and they are outside. They come by simple emails, through phishing, and via even more sophisticated carefully customized spear phishing attacks. They are directed, typically, at people, all of whom, under the right set of circumstances, are vulnerable to skilled social engineering or to a momentary lapse in prudence and judgment. They come from malware that learns on the fly. They come from malware that seeks patterns of data and that operates completely autonomously until it finds its treasure and then calls home.

Although good cybersecurity, including the application of all security patches and updates, reduces the fraction of attacks that result in a breach, over the long term, both threats and breaches are impossible to prevent. So, what can you do?

With absolute prevention off the table, the goal of always being able to stop, evade, avoid, or otherwise defeat every attack is now unrealistic. It is no longer enough to have the highest, thickest, strongest wall along the perimeter of your network. In fact, we are so intensively and extensively interconnected, and we rely so thoroughly on connectedness, that we cannot afford to cower behind our walls. A security strategy that cuts us off from threats also cuts us off from business itself. What we need is to defend our networks as best we can with good technology, policies, and practices, but we must also be able to identify incidents when they begin and have the knowledge of how a particular incident is attacking us. To gain this intelligence, we need to know our network as intimately as we know the layout of our office or home. This means upping our cyberdefense capability with digital resilience as a core tenet of our cybersecurity strategy.

This is not a choice. It is a necessity. We are in a new era in which the best prevention and protection systems—no matter how extraordinarily sophisticated—are incapable of keeping all the bad guys out. The public sees evidence of this practically every week in news reports. And what the *public* sees is a mere fraction of what is reported daily in the security industry media. Indeed, many organizations are not legally required to report breaches, and many therefore go unreported. The volume and the effectiveness of the threats are not due to the carelessness of businesses, government, and other institutions (although sometimes these users are very careless). It is not because IT folks do not know how to run their security systems. (They do.) It is not because the security industry produces bad products. (They produce some of the best products that have ever been available.) The success of today's threats comes from the fact that the bad guys have figured out how to engineer attacks that get inside the network through normally open doors, even when the network has walls, guards, access control, and encryption.

Resilience is a strategy that admits this fact without surrendering to it.

URGENT—MOST BUSINESS NETWORKS LACK RESILIENCE

I have invested a good many words in this book defining and discussing resilience. My purpose has been to show that, far from a novel concept, resilience is the way people, businesses, governments, nations, institutions, biological organisms, and ecosystems have been surviving and thriving for untold centuries. It is more recent reality that has me worried. I have observed, over the last several decades, that we have rarely applied resilience strategies to our digital networks.

Our digital networks are under unprecedented threat today. Resilience, as applied to them, can be thought of simply as the capability of containing an incident and taking swift action before the whole network or organization is compromised. While the threat is contained, the network can withstand the attack and continue to operate even as the users of the network go about eliminating the threat. Once the attack is over or the threat has been defeated, a resilience strategy also prescribes a program of recovery that includes learning from the attack and hardening the network accordingly.

Remember, it isn't as if resilience is an alien concept. Contemporary society is so focused on resilience that our government has an organization like the National Transportation Safety Board (NTSB) to review air and other transportation disasters, discover what went wrong, and give the industry feedback on how to make things better, more resilient, and therefore safer for us all. Resilience is so important to us that we take organizations like the NTSB pretty much for granted. Yet nothing like this exists on the digital network, even though half of all businesses talk to their customers primarily or exclusively through that network. They are, primarily or exclusively, digital businesses.

As I explained in Chapter 2, resilience is even part of the heritage, the DNA, of the Internet. At its inception, Internet architecture incorporated certain inherently resilient features. That historical fact, added to the many examples of resilience we have in the analog world, makes even more flabbergasting and frustrating the fact that most of today's digital networks are being designed with little or no resilience in mind.

HOW TO ADDRESS THE GREAT WEAKNESS OF TODAY'S BUSINESS NETWORKS

The great weakness of networks today is the absence of holistic, systemic thinking that goes into the typical vast and costly corporate network. It is a structure that has usually grown over time and therefore consists of hundreds, thousands, or even hundreds of thousands of different devices from a spectrum of more than a hundred different vendors. Each device has a specific, critical function. The result is an interconnected assemblage that is piecemeal and uncoordinated.

Moreover, most security products are just as atomized as the other elements of today's typical network. A particular security product may deal with the firewall, for instance, or with a host computer. But what we really need are network components and security products that are designed with the entire network in mind. The old saying about a chain being only as strong as its weakest link is very true of digital networks. Ninety-nine robust components and one vulnerable component do not add up to a network that is 99 percent resilient and just 1 percent vulnerable. The sum of 99 + 1 in this instance is a nonresilient network, period. In fact, the compromise in resilience may be enormous—way beyond what the 99 *robust* versus 1 *vulnerable* ratio might suggest. Think of a large, complex network as a big, sophisticated live spreadsheet loaded with formulas. Change something in cell B-25, and it may affect the content of E-18 or D-12 or C-5 or any combination of these and more. But imagine that *you* didn't even build this spreadsheet. You have no idea what formulas are connected to what cells. Networks these days have many authors, and many of those original designers are long gone. So, it's no wonder you don't know what happens in cell C-5 if you change the value in cell B-25. Or in the case of a digital network, change a router configuration in Spokane, which will have an impact elsewhere in the network—in Spokane or Poughkeepsie or Kathmandu.

ACTION ITEM

Start treating your network as you would a spreadsheet for a complex and critically important P&L. Know that if you change something in cell B-25, it will affect other cells, other operations, other outcomes, and maybe even the bottom line. It may distort the entire spreadsheet—perhaps catastrophically. But even if the change makes the spreadsheet just a little wrong, is this acceptable?

If you don't know how that router change will affect your network, you cannot design for resilience. If your heterogeneous collection of components were not each designed to work optimally together in the first place, you cannot now design for resilience. Look, we have already admitted that the Internet is unbelievably complex, its complexity only partly defined by nodes numbered in the trillions. You cannot do anything about the resilience of the Internet. You can, however, introduce resilience into your particular node on that Internet, your system, your network inside your firewall(s). The first step toward this is to understand your network. To gain this understanding, you need a comprehensive, accurate, and up-to-date overview of the entire network. I don't mean a simple flat plat with symbols connected by lines as on a paper roadmap. I'm talking about a dynamic model, in which the symbols have a unique configuration and the lines represent specific traffic types and flows. You can still think of it as something like a map if you like, but it is more akin to a Google map with the underlying street, lane, directionality, and near real-time traffic information. With a model like this, you can make a meaningful judgment about the resilience of the whole network, not just its disparate parts.

There are software tools available that provide this kind of complete, current picture of your network. Full disclosure: This is where my own company comes in. At RedSeal we have created an enterprise-class software capable of building a network model across even the largest organizations, able to perform diagnostics and to provide measurements telling you where the problems are. Most important, it will tell you if you are making your network better, more resilient, as time passes. RedSeal provides measurements that show you how the heterogeneous elements of your network actually operate together and just how this interoperation produces or fails to produce increasing digital resilience based on your organization's policies and designs.

No matter how different they may be, each component in your network does have at least one thing in common. Every one of them includes configuration software that allows the component to operate on the network. Software such as RedSeal's network modeling and risk-scoring platform reads the configuration files from your network devices and applies diagnostics that, based on years of experience and vendor information designed into it, renders a judgment about how well or poorly each device is configured to operate in your environment. This configuration data is then loaded into our enterprise modeling software, which builds a network map—or, more precisely, a software model of your network. This gives you an overall view of the network as it exists right now.

WHY YOU NEED TO GET TO KNOW YOUR NETWORK

There is nothing new about mapping a network. Indeed, most companies or institutions have such maps and there are numerous products, many of them free, that give you a "picture" of a network. But pictures are flat, dead flat, in fact. Usually, they depict only how the network was initially built. They do not reflect its inevitable evolution over time as devices are added, subtracted, or otherwise modified and as users join or leave. Further complicating this evolution are changes beyond devices and users, as instances of virtual or cloud networks are accessed, and as technologies such as Amazon Web Services (AWS) are used to set up cloud-based servers on demand. The cloud has brought to many business networks connections that the organization's IT department may not even know about. What is required is a picture as close to real-time as possible, a network model that is continually refreshed to create a dynamic map for a dynamic system that changes profoundly whenever something is added, changed, or taken off the network.

ACTION ITEM

Use network modeling software to create a full, frequently refreshed map of your network and all its connections. Static maps drawn when your network was first designed are as useful in understanding your network today as a map of Caesar's Rome is useful in navigating the streets of modern Rome.

All organizations have corporate policies pertaining to their networks and their operations. In addition, governments and industry associations impose regulatory policies, such as NERC CIP, or PCI DSS for the electrical power industry, or HIPAA in healthcare. And there are organizational policies that dictate who gets what from where and how they can reach that information. With a network model, these diverse policies can be tested. If they prove not to be compliant, a good model will offer suggestions to make them compliant. A *really* good model will also allow you to test those suggestions for effect and effectiveness. For example, a simple policy barring a classified network from communicating with an unclassified network should be readily testable with a network model. Or consider the PCI DSS policy. Every company with customer payment card information on the Internet has to abide by it, and it is complicated. Nevertheless, it can be fully expressed in a model that everyone can understand. And yes, there are policies, including PCI DSS, that require audits. The ability to image your network as it currently exists will help you to ensure that your network policies are in place and performing as they are designed to. A dynamic map will tell you when reality drifts out of alignment with policies, letting you know if you have a problem before the audit begins.

THINK LESS ABOUT YOUR NETWORK, THINK MORE ABOUT YOUR DATA.

Today's networks do not stop at the perimeter of your property. No analytical mapping software is adequate if it fails to extend the network model through the physical network to your virtual network and your cloud-based network. Creating and maintaining resilience requires understanding and controlling connections to the outside and access to the connections on the inside.

The phrase "access to your network" is fairly meaningless. What matters is access to your *data*—and even this phrase does not convey the whole story. Some data should be accessible to just about anybody who wants it. Other data needs to be protected from casual access by the public, vendors, partners, or customers. Indeed, not every employee connected to your internal network should have access to every category of data. So, the only meaningful way to plan "access" is to define categories of data, prioritize the categories in terms of degree of access that should be allowed, and segment your network accordingly. Just as it makes no sense to grant public access to your most sensitive data, it is also destructive to your business to arbitrarily restrict access to data that your customers need, the general public needs, or most of your employees most of the time need. Security is about security. Resilience is about business. A resilient business provides *degrees* of access that promote productive access to data crucial to promotion, presentation, and transaction while jealously guarding access to prized intellectual property and sensitive financial data. The structure of the network needs to accommodate such crucial differentiation.

Dynamic modeling of your network must include a reliable vulnerability scan that will allow you to perform network triage by creating a priority list of vulnerabilities for the whole system, not just for specific devices. It is often the case that a host or computer with a severe vulnerability may be well protected by good network architecture, but a host or computer with a less severe vulnerability is directly connected to an untrusted router. Common sense dictates that you fix the severe vulnerability first. But common sense does not always yield the most effective strategy. Sophisticated modeling and risk-scoring software identifies known software vulnerabilities on the devices in a network. Good management systems score the severity of the vulnerability and determine what kind of data is on a device. The nature of the data is critical to determining its value. (Databases, for instance, are high-value assets.) Traditionally, prioritization has been based on vulnerability severity and on the value of the data asset. This view almost always results in a list of vulnerabilities far too numerous to patch or otherwise address.

The RedSeal model, for example, adds a third dimension to the triage, the element of accessibility. How reachable are the vulnerabilities via untrusted networks? And just what can be reached, should a given device be compromised? By answering these questions, you have the ability to model your network the way a skilled combat commander models a battlefield—not just in one-dimensional terms of simple vulnerability, but in degree of vulnerability, relative value of assets, and accessibility of assets. If you know how and where your network is exposed, and you have a complete and granular understanding of the value consequences of the exposure, you know what areas to harden and what areas to attend to first.

ACTION ITEMS

Digital resilience begins with deep knowledge of your data and your networks. Using the best available modeling and scoring tools, build this knowledge by—

1. Verifying that device configurations comply with relevant regulations and industry best practices.
2. Modeling your network as it exists at this moment—in other words, collecting configuration and operation data of your network devices as often as you deem necessary and without burdening your network.
3. Visualizing end-to-end access and path details, so that you see intended as well as unintended access among all the parts of your network. You need to know what access paths exist from the Internet into your network. Are all access paths authorized? Do any—authorized or not—expose privileged or sensitive areas of your network to external threats?
4. Measuring your network resilience. You cannot manage what you cannot measure; therefore, measurement is essential.
5. Identifying hidden areas of your network—the "scary parts" of your network, areas you don't even know exist. These can be significant security risks.
6. Prioritizing vulnerability patching. A map—even a live and accurate map—of your network is not enough. You need to triage your vulnerabilities so that you can allocate resources to first patch those in most urgent need of attention—based on the network situation, not on the absolute value of the vulnerable asset.

7. Verifying network security policy. You need to know if your security policies are being implemented as specified. This is essential information for assessing the real resilience of your network. A security policy is meaningless unless it is implemented. In fact, it is worse than meaningless, because it is deceptive. This exposes you to both operational and legal liabilities. The most basic knowledge managers need is knowing what they know as well as what they do not know about their networks. No state of ignorance is more potentially destructive that not knowing what you do not know.
8. Prioritizing network change control. You need the capability to assess the security impact of potential or proposed changes to your network. Model the changes you want before you implement them to ensure that you do not cause unintended issues. Perform virtual penetration testing to identify unintended access and other issues. By testing proposed configurations and conducting penetration testing, you get the information you need to optimize your existing cyber investments.

WHAT HAPPENS WHEN NOBODY PRIORITIZES THE DATA

Back in 2010, Chelsea Elizabeth Manning was a U.S. Army private named Bradley Manning, an intelligence analyst who, as he explained in a message to threat analyst and self-confessed convicted hacker Adrian Lamo, "deployed to eastern Baghdad, pending discharge for 'adjustment disorder' in lieu of [his actual medical complaint,] 'gender identity disorder.'" Put another way, Manning was a soldier of the lowest possible rank who had been placed in a highly sensitive position even though he was slated for discharge after revealing (as he told Lamo) "my uncertainty over my gender identity." His security clearance gave him what he described as "free reign [*sic*] over classified networks for long periods of time." He told Lamo that he saw "incredible things, awful things . . . things that belonged in the public domain, and not on some server stored in a dark room in Washington DC"—yet things that were fully accessible to him in an outpost in Iraq.[2]

In April 2010, Manning disclosed to WikiLeaks, the organization that publishes secret information, news leaks, and classified media from anonymous sources, almost three-quarters of a million classified or sensitive military and diplomatic documents. He was subsequently tried for and convicted of (among other offenses) stealing government secrets. (Sentenced to thirty-five years imprisonment in August 2013 for the WikiLeaks disclosures, Manning was released on May 17, 2017, pursuant to a commutation by President Barack Obama.[3]) In legal terms, the charge of "theft of government documents" may be completely accurate. In practical terms, however, Manning didn't so much steal the secrets as the U.S. Army left them out for the taking. The army had set itself up for the breach either by failing to understand the end-to-end access points of its own networks or by failing to appreciate the potential consequences of how the network was laid out.

Ask yourself: What need did a remote firebase in Iraq have for full access to confidential information, including diplomatic information, stored in suburban Washington on Pentagon servers? Intelligent, timely network modeling and a prudent, practical access policy might have prevented the Manning-WikiLeaks breach. In this case, the weakness in the network was less a matter of digital technology than of mismanaged—or perhaps unmanaged—clearance policies. A low-ranking and poorly performing soldier in an outlying base should never have had access to Pentagon plums. Yet accurate, dynamic network modeling would very likely have surfaced this error in policy, and a good digital posture of resilience might well have prevented the Manning-WikiLeaks breach.

TIME TO GET YOUR HEAD INTO THE CLOUD

Today's networks typically integrate with cloud systems. It is vitally important to visualize your network *including* its cloud integration to ensure that these make for a single resilient system that protects you and your customers. You also need to go even farther beyond your own network. You can do little about the security of the Internet, but more and more companies are demanding the capability of assessing and certifying the security of any part of their supply chain that accesses their network. Recall the Target breach discussed in Chapter 1. The origin of the breach was the compromise of an HVAC vendor that served many Target stores. It is true that Target's corporate network was not properly segmented from its point-of-sale system. That lapse in resilience and security was on Target. However, the HVAC vendor's network was also insufficiently hardened.

As Target discovered to its dismay as well as that of many of its customers, its network was at least as risky as the riskiest element in its supply chain. When everything is connected, it becomes imperative that companies demand that their suppliers confirm a secure environment. A thorough, accurate, dynamic network analysis can provide that confirmation or indicate what needs to be addressed to achieve a level of security and resilience sufficient to certify adequate compliance.

HOW TO SCORE NETWORK RESILIENCE

"You don't need a weatherman / To know which way the wind blows," 2016 Nobel laureate Bob Dylan told us in "Subterranean Homesick Blues" back in 1965.[4] Today, in the second decade of the twenty-first century, we don't need technologists, sociologists, or the authors of *Trillions* to know that intensive, pervasive, universal digital networking has blown our world into a zone of unprecedented complexity. We work it, and we live it. We cannot evade or escape, let alone deny, the ubiquitous complexity.

A trillion Internet nodes and more is a trillion too many units of complexity to evade, escape, or deny. So maybe Hollywood can help. In the 2015 big-screen blockbuster *The Martian,* astronaut Matt Damon finds himself going solo on the surface of Mars after his crew, swept up in the mother of all dust storms, leaves him for dead and blasts off for home 33.9 million miles away. As an article in *Business Insider* (yes, *Business Insider*) asks, "How do you survive on an inhospitable planet when you're stranded there alone?" Well, you don't try to escape, evade, or deny reality. *Business Insider* quotes the marooned astronaut himself: "In the face of overwhelming odds, I'm left with only one option. I'm going to have to science the shit out of this."[5]

Ideally, software tools built to map and analyze your network will not only accurately represent the complexity of the structure and all its devices and connections, but will also "science the shit out of it" with the object of reducing an incredibly complex analysis to something readily comprehensible—not just to IT experts, but to nontechnical C-suite leadership as well. While other companies use different scoring methods, RedSeal uses a numerical score modeled on the familiar "credit score" measure of consumer credit risk.

Let me explain. In the pre-digital days of consumer credit lending, banks and businesses evaluated creditworthiness on "The Three Cs," namely Character, Capital, and Capacity. Capital (real estate, personal property, investments, savings, etc.) and Capacity (ability to repay, namely income) are directly calculable using arithmetical methods, even if it's, say, 1930, and all you have is pencil, paper, or maybe one of those adding machines with a big-handled pull lever.

But the very first consideration, the one given pride of place among those Three Cs, Character, is not readily calculable. Doubtless, some banks and lenders made attempts to score a credit applicant's Character by assigning points for certain actions, virtues, and vices revealed in her personal history. Nevertheless, in the end, the evaluation of Character is a human decision, which, like all human decisions is largely subjective and, therefore, complex. The decision process must often have been subject to wrangling within the lending firm. Unquestionably, some applicants were disappointed, dismayed, or just plain pissed concerning the outcome. Likely, they let their displeasure be known. The lender's rationale for a given credit decision could be presented as a combination of numbers (in the case of the second two Cs) and human judgment (in the case of the first C). There was demonstrable transparency in the second two Cs, but it would be difficult to rule out the presence of irrational subjectivity or outright bias in the evaluation of an applicant's Character. The inherent complexity of this part of the judgment must have seemed irreducible, at least in the pre-digital age.

The credit *score*, a product of the era of digital financial record keeping, sought to finally reduce it all to numbers and then to reduce those numbers to a single number. Like the details of the formula for Coca-Cola, the formulas used to calculate the most widely used brand of credit score are trade secrets and jealously guarded. But the rough composition of that score is open-source knowledge.[6]

- 35 percent is payment history
- 30 percent is debt burden
- 15 percent is length of credit history
- 10 percent is types of credit used
- 10 percent is recent searches for credit (mainly "hard credit inquiries," the kind that occur when a consumer applies for a credit card or loan)

Arguably, the commonly used credit scoring systems set out to "science the shit out of the complexity" involved in evaluating creditworthiness by simply ignoring the first C, Character. Based on what little we know about the rationale behind proprietary credit scoring systems, it is just as arguable that they do quantify everything that can be quantified concerning Character. Payment history, the length of credit history, and the types of credit used all speak in some way to Character. In any case, all credit scoring systems introduce into credit decisions a level of objectivity and transparency that was unavailable in the pre-digital Three Cs model. In emulating the credit score model, RedSeal has sought to introduce similar qualities into a network resilience score.

In the RedSeal system, the higher the score the greater the likelihood that the networks of the business evaluated are sufficiently resilient to withstand a cyber incident and keep running. If you do things to your network that raise your score, you know that you are increasing its cyber resilience. If you do things that lower it, you know that you are making your networks less resilient. The RedSeal Digital Resilience Score is based on three broad components:

1. How well you know what your digital infrastructure looks like; for this, you need a dynamic model.
2. How well your network equipment is configured.
3. Vulnerability of your computing devices in the context of the network—that is, situational awareness. For example, the software evaluates the presence of known issues and their severity; the location of these issues, including the value of the asset associated with them; and whether the asset in question can be reached directly from the outside or from another vulnerable asset. At the end of the day, this allows you to prioritize the weaknesses in the resilience of the network and focus on them.

These three components contribute to a numerical score, which is intended to aid in evaluating network resilience by resolving complexity without distorting or disguising the salient issues. Using this score, we can harden the soft parts of a network and evaluate the impact of this hardening with a number rather than with speculative narrative analysis. Any transaction, no matter how inherently simple or complex, is made more complicated if more than one language is being spoken in negotiation. Finding a single, common, mutually intelligible language productively simplifies any transaction. In business, the lingua franca is money, which is expressed in numbers. A numerical resilience score does for network resilience what money does for business. It offers a common language by which resilience may be unambiguously evaluated.

With a resilience score, the allocation of funds (input) and the cost-benefit analysis of their application (output) are made significantly more straightforward. For instance: Your company's chief financial officer (CFO) sees a resilience score of 450. The chief information security officer (CISO) wants $100 million to raise the resilience score to 600. Based on the score, the CFO can evaluate this request by modeling the proposed 100 million dollars' worth of changes to the network to see how these impact the resilience score. Maybe it will take just $50 million to move the needle to 600—or to 550, which is judged to be good enough for now. Maybe $100 million will fail to push that needle far enough. Whatever the outcome of the what-if modeling, the CFO can produce a judgment expressed in the language of business, in which all the denizens of the C-suite are fluent.

This is in stark contrast to the typical way in which a CISO makes his budget request—by calling for so many additional firewalls, *X* more antivirus packages, several additional fire intrusion detection systems, and so on. To nontechnical executives, an inventory of hardware and software is fairly meaningless. It is the CISO saying to them, *Just take my word for it. We need it.* Far more meaningful to most of the C-suite is to be told what *outcome* the requested funds will produce. Nontechnical executives need a practical way to talk about and evaluate cost versus benefit. It is not a case of technical people dumbing down the details for nontechnical people. It is a case in which everyone must find and speak a common language that tells the truth clearly and without evasion, distortion, or denial.

EVALUATE THE NETWORKS TO WHICH YOUR NETWORK CONNECTS

As mentioned earlier, it is not sufficient to gain knowledge of your network and only your network. You must also go outside of your own network to assess those to which you are connected. Based on this assessment, you may make changes to your network to harden it appropriately, you may demand that a prospective vendor (for instance) harden its network, or you may do both. As a lender would use some form of credit score to assess the creditworthiness of a prospective borrower before making a loan, so too can you use resilience scores to evaluate a prospective vendor or other key business partners before they connect. Similarly, if your organization is looking to acquire another company, a critical part of your due diligence must be an assessment of your two networks. Suppose your network has a resilience score of 650, and you score the network of the company marked for acquisition at just 475. The awful truth is that you are buying a network riskier than yours. Connect to that network, and the resulting total score will drop. By scoring the target company's network, you can model the impact of that acquisition before you sign, and you can make your decisions accordingly. If you decide to proceed with the acquisition and the resulting connection, you have a basis for negotiating or renegotiating a fair price as well as liability escrow provisions and contingencies.

Knowing your network is a vital element in the due diligence phase of acquisition as well as in your own daily operations. On July 25, 2016, Verizon Communications announced its intention to acquire the Internet business of Yahoo for $4.83 billion. On the face of it, that seemed a bargain-basement price for a company that had been valued at $100 billion back in the late 2000s, when it was the most popular American website.[7] But then came Thursday, September 22, 2016, the day Yahoo announced that "the account information of at least 500 million users" had been stolen by hackers—stolen two years earlier, in 2014.[8] That was bad until it got worse. On December 14, 2016, the company announced that "more than 1 billion accounts" had been breached, not in 2014, but in 2013.[9] The 2014 hack came to light only after 200 million Yahoo accounts were discovered for sale on a "darknet market" website called TheRealDeal.[10] The 2013 breach came to light as a result of another darknet black market sales revelation.[11]

Most businesses would be keenly aware of losing 1.5 billion of anything, and probably within a fairly short time of the loss. In the case of the Yahoo breaches, however, the loss was discovered only after the purloined data was put up for sale. One thing was quite clear. Yahoo managers had considerably less than perfect knowledge of their network.

But if the compromise of 1.5 billion users came as a long-delayed surprise to Yahoo, it was an instant stunner for Verizon. That company was on the precipice of making Yahoo's problems its own by purchasing them for $4.83 billion; however, on December 15, 2016, *Bloomberg Technology* reported that Verizon was exploring revising the purchase price downward or simply walking away from Yahoo altogether. In the end, although significantly delayed by the fallout from disclosure of the two data breaches, the deal closed on June 8, 2017 for $4.48 billion.[12]

ACTION ITEM

Your network is only as secure and resilient as the networks with which you connect. Before establishing a working connection with another company—a vendor, a customer, a prospective partner or acquisition—thoroughly evaluate the security and resilience of the company's networks. Merge with an insecure network, and the insecurity becomes yours.

Mergers and acquisitions have always involved risk—not just the risk that the investment might simply fail to pan out, but that instead of acquiring a valuable asset, you might find yourself saddled with a ruinous liability—say, a shopping mall built on a sinkhole or intellectual property that was not patented properly. M&A in the digital age offers opportunity and risk compounded. You don't just acquire digital assets, you also risk acquiring a network of undetected digital liabilities. The breach revelations that came close to wrecking the Verizon-Yahoo merger may have been late in coming, but they were not too late. They came before the deal was closed. It takes no strategy whatsoever to dodge a bullet, just a lot of luck. And Verizon was indeed lucky, because neither it nor Yahoo seems to have had an effective strategy for assessing the resilience of the Yahoo network. Well, luck's certainly a wonderful thing—as long as you are lucky enough to have it. The trouble is, of all the good things you can have, luck is the least resilient. You just cannot rely on it. One universal truth applies to all business and, indeed, to all human endeavor. There is no reward without risk. Get up out of bed, let your feet hit the floor, take a step, and there is a risk that you will fall, plant your face in the floor, and break your nose. Fail to take that step, however, and you forgo any opportunity the dawning day holds. Our intensively connected world offers an unprecedented array of potentially rewarding opportunities as well as an unprecedented array of risks. No connected enterprise can permanently avoid the risk of cyberattack, but it can take measures to manage the risk.

ACTION ITEMS

In terms of your networks, here are the key questions you and your risk officer need to ask in order to manage risk effectively:

1. What audit policies do we have in place? How effective are these policies? How can we confirm that these policies—which may be effective in theory—are actually in force as stated?
2. Do we understand our networks? That is, do we have a comprehensive capability of managing our digital enterprise from the point of view of risk?
3. What are we paying for our cyber insurance? Is it enough? Or is it too much?

The ability to present a resilience score as well a model of your network should help you determine your needs and put you in a more advantageous position to negotiate the best possible premium. Demonstrating lower risk is, after all, a strong argument for securing a lower premium.

GIVE DIGITAL RESILIENCE A GOOD SEAT AT THE MANAGEMENT TABLE

In 2005, futurist Thomas L. Friedman published *The World Is Flat: A Brief History of the Twenty-first Century*.[13] The book globally extended the vision of a trend that was already strong in many business organizations as early as the 1970s: the transformation of hierarchies and silos into flatter and flatter corporate organizations. Today, we see this most particularly and most dramatically in how technology has emerged from the back office to envelop not only the entire enterprise but to reach far beyond the walls of any organization. Technology has gone a long way toward making business seamless, borderless, with barely a separation between producer and consumer, and often with nary a brick rising from the flat earth.

This is today's business landscape. Everything is brought forward. The network can no longer by regarded as the exclusive preserve of "IT." Of course, we need the tech experts, but IT also needs a seat at the management table, and a CISO or other cybersecurity executive belongs in the boardroom too, just as boards today have executives for compensation, audit, and other key functions. The presence of IT and cybersecurity at the highest management levels requires those executives and the others to be fully fluent in the same language. The most natural language *for* business is the language *of* business, which is money. Revenues, expenses, profits, taxes, you name it, numbers are the actionable measure by which all business strategy, debate, and decisions begin, pull apart, come back together, and productively conclude.

TAKEAWAY

The universal "Catch-22" of business today is that connectivity, a business necessity, creates vulnerability. Fortunately, good, continuously updated cybersecurity reduces the rate at which cyberattacks are converted into actual breaches. Nevertheless, security alone prevents neither attacks nor breaches. Make no mistake, perimeter defenses are absolutely mandatory, but they are also insufficient against today's threats. Think beyond digital security to create digital resilience. This begins with knowing your network as intimately as you know the layout of your office or home. Resilience also requires recognition that no network or network component is an island. You need to evaluate all networks with which you establish a working connection. Vulnerabilities in the network of a vendor, customer, partner, or acquisition become the vulnerabilities of your network. As for network components, change or reconfigure one device, and it can affect your entire network.

- Employ policies and technologies that allow you to understand the impact of each change *before* you make the change.
- Prioritize your data in terms of accessibility versus the need to restrict access.
- Build (or rebuild) the structure of your network accordingly.

7

RESILIENT RESPONSE

Making Resilience a Whole-Business, Whole-Nation, Whole-World Issue

For most business people at a C-suite or board level, the technical guts of the Internet to which they and their businesses connect might as well be the dark matter of the universe. Astrophysicists tell us that dark matter makes up about 84.5 percent of *total* mass. Add dark energy to dark matter, and you have accounted for 95.1 percent of the *total* mass-energy content of the *total* universe.[1] Concerning this 95.1 percent, we know next to nothing because it is dark. Our own little slice of the Internet, our personal or corporate local area network (LAN) and, perhaps, wide area network (WAN), are not so grand a mystery as dark matter and dark energy, but most of those whose very livelihood depends on them have little insight into the network or networks they own (or at least pay for) and control (or at least believe they do).

Like 95.1 percent of the universe, these technologies are black boxes: data in, data out, that is all ye know on earth, and all ye need to know. Such is the view too many corporate and institutional IT managers, C-suite executives, and boards of directors have accepted and even encouraged for far too long. Only the geeks, anointed acolytes of digital technology, know how the channels work, just what the *something* is, and exactly *where* it goes. The thing is, in all too many companies and other organizations, even the geeks may not have a complete understanding of how the black boxes work, what they convey, and where they convey it. Even if they do, they often neither know or much care about the *purpose* of what is conveyed.

This is the disconnect in many of today's intensively connected businesses. The techies know (though not always as much as they think they know) the *what* and the *how* of the networks under their stewardship, but they do not know or care nearly as much about the *why*. As for CEOs, boards, investors, and corporate stakeholders of all kinds, the *why* is the *only* thing they care about.

ACTION ITEM

Achieving digital resilience begins with knowledge. The less you know about your networks—where they connect, how they connect, to whom they give access, and what they expose—the less resilient your networks and the organization they support. Get inside the black box. Empower and enable the C-suite and board to communicate with the IT professionals and vice versa. Digital infrastructure and operations must be treated as whole-business matters, not mere technical issues. Digital resilience is a business value.

MAKE DIGITAL RESILIENCE A TOP WHOLE-BUSINESS PRIORITY

"Backward-looking." That is what the authors of an excellent book on the role of digital resilience in business, *Beyond Cybersecurity: Protecting Your Digital Business,* call the critical structural disconnect that exists in most of today's corporate enterprises: the sharp division between technology personnel and C-suite leaders. These authors explain that as "recently as seven or eight years ago" (writing in 2015), "cybersecurity was not a priority for many companies. . . . What protections existed were focused on defending the perimeter of the corporate network, and IT security organizations' role was to manage tools such as remote access and antivirus software." As for non-IT personnel, CEOs, managers, and frontline employees, they "faced few consequences for violating security policies."[2]

Things have changed in those seven or eight years. Technology executives report "that they have made significant progress in establishing cybersecurity as a control function." They have brought cybersecurity into the C-suite in the form of the CISO. They have created programs to educate employees about phishing exploits in an earnest effort to prevent employees having their credentials stolen or inadvertently introducing malware into company networks. They have formulated network architecture standards to segment access to help prevent infiltrations like the one that occurred in the Target attack, which was successful in part because of an improperly segmented network (Chapter 1). Thanks to improvements in software development, especially continuous software security, CISOs can report that security flaws in bespoke as well as off-the-shelf software are typically identified earlier and remediated very quickly by the timely distribution of patches.[3]

ACTION ITEMS

Resilience is not a synonym for *security.* Both are necessary, and neither, by itself, is sufficient to manage the business risks created by digital networks. In the pursuit of resilience, do not neglect the basics of security:

- Make cybersecurity a C-suite issue.
- Give cybersecurity a seat at the management table and in the boardroom in the person of a CISO (Chief Information Security Officer) or the equivalent.
- Institute programs to educate employees about safe computing, with an emphasis on avoiding phishing exploits.
- Establish, as components of business policy, network architecture standards that segment access to help prevent intrusions and consequent breaches with exfiltration of intellectual property and other data.
- Adopt state-of-the art continuous software security, so that software vulnerabilities can be identified early and remediated quickly.
- Make the deployment and installation of software security updates and patches an absolute doctrine of business policy.
- Share, throughout the organization and the business community, information concerning threats and breaches.

The *Beyond Cybersecurity* authors correctly point out that, while establishing "cybersecurity as a control function was . . . necessary

[and] . . . dramatically reduced risk for a great many institutions, . . . it is less and less tenable as the threat of cyberattacks continue[s] to rise." The control function approach puts the responsibility for security on the cybersecurity/IT team and nowhere else. Based on attacks that have happened somewhere at some earlier time, the approach "tries to protect against yesterday's attacks." It tends as well to rely on manual interventions and inspections, so it has limited scalability.[4] The result is that most of our businesses and institutions are not as secure as they could and must be. Even worse, our enterprises suffer from increased "tension between cybersecurity and the innovation and flexibility craved by the business."[5] Traditionally, non-IT security types have complained that cybersecurity requirements slow things down and are therefore bad for business. Despite improvements, the current state of cybersecurity often delivers the worst of two worlds: inadequate security *plus* hobbled innovation and agility.

Businesses find themselves in the unenviable position of making steps toward cybersecurity without achieving markedly improved security. Worse, the steps they take impede critical aspects of their business. If leaders of such businesses find themselves in pain, they can attribute their acute discomfort to the fact that they are sitting on a tipping point.

I know what they need to do to get relief.

They need to move forward. They need to grab the problem and execute a solution. They need to tip. This means admitting that they have taken cybersecurity as far as it can be taken and that the time has now come to go beyond cybersecurity and work instead toward achieving digital resilience.

RATIONALIZE THE DATA PRIORITIES OF YOUR BUSINESS

There are specific technological steps companies can take to harden their networks (and I will consider these in a few moments), but the transition from the goal of cybersecurity to the goal of digital resilience requires evaluating and understanding the data priorities and structures of your business to rationalize them for both business efficiency and security. The process of prioritizing begins with understanding the urgent imperative of integrating cybersecurity directly and thoroughly into the way you do business, to fold it into all your business processes, and to promote it as a key aspect of your value proposition. Indeed, the cardinal distinction between digital resilience and cybersecurity is that digital resilience is what results when cybersecurity is thoroughly integrated into everything the business does instead of just slapped on at the end.

ACTION ITEM

Cybersecurity cannot provide absolute security because absolute security is incompatible with networked interactivity. In other words, absolute security is incompatible with business. Hedge risk by means of good cybersecurity, then move forward to achieving digital resilience, which is about business rather than security. Surviving and thriving in today's intensively networked business environment requires policies and procedures that balance security with resilience.

The *Beyond Cybersecurity* authors enumerate what they call seven "hallmarks of digital resilience."[6] They are worth summarizing here—with comments—because they do in fact contribute to resilience and, even more, because they demonstrate that digital resilience is not just an IT issue, a network security issue, a hardware security issue, or a software security issue. Resilience is a business issue that begins with prioritizing your data assets across your networks.

1. *"Prioritize information assets based on business risks."* Cybersecurity teams should work with executives and managers across the business to prioritize business data assets. Such prioritization is neither strictly a digital security issue nor a business issue. It is an indivisible blend of the two.

   We must add a caveat, however. Avoid excessively simplifying the process of translating digital data risks into business risks. As discussed in Chapter 6, modeling and scoring capabilities such as those RedSeal provides make prioritization more granular and therefore more useful by assessing not only the business value of data items and their vulnerability from a technical standpoint, but also adding to the analysis the likelihood of attack and the relative accessibility of each data asset.
2. *"Provide differentiated protection for the most important assets."* This follows directly from #1. Aligning the level of protection provided to a set of information assets with the business importance of those assets seems like a self-evident principle. Yet relatively few businesses go through with this assessment. Extremely sensitive or critical data warrants special protections such as a high level of encryption and multifactor authentication, whereas such steps would be overkill for less critical data. Insofar as such overkill slows or otherwise impedes important business processes—es-

pecially those processes involving customer or client interaction—they harm the business rather than meaningfully enhance security.

3. *"Integrate cybersecurity into enterprise-wide risk management and governance processes."* Cybersecurity is no longer an adjunct to business, it is "intertwined with almost all of an institution's major business processes." This means that "product development, marketing and sales, supply chain, corporate affairs, human resources (HR), and risk management" are all bound up with cybersecurity. Cybersecurity is, simply, everyone's business.

   Supply chain may be singled out as especially critical in the current business environment. Target (Chapter 1) is just one of many businesses that discovered the peril lurking in its supply chain as the insecurity of a B2B contractor's digital network enabled the penetration of Target's network.

   Expect more and more businesses to require specific cybersecurity certifications from prospective vendors and contractors. The upside of this for proactive companies is that they can seize the opportunity to promote their high level of certifiable cybersecurity practices as a benefit and value added.

4. *"Enlist frontline personnel to protect the information assets they use."* Digital resilience is achieved from the top down as well as from the bottom up. While cybersecurity experts must fully enlist CEOs and boards of directors in integrating digital resilience throughout the business, employees at every level must be recruited to protect whatever data assets they handle. This is especially critical in the case of customer-facing personnel.

5. *"Integrate cybersecurity into the technology environment."* Cybersecurity should not be considered an add-on to the technologies the business uses or creates, but, rather, integral to their design. The trend toward building inherently secure software—software developed using thoroughly vetted modules and subject to continuous monitoring and continuous development—is an example of such continuous integration.
6. *"Deploy active defenses to engage attackers."* The era of total reliance on a Maginot Line or Chinese Wall approach to cybersecurity, the passive defense of network perimeters and network segments, has fled. In today's threat environment, a proactive approach is required. Companies need to maintain a high level of awareness informed by multiple intelligence sources. Collect the data, analyze the data, and adjust countermeasures accordingly.
7. *"Test continuously to improve incident response across business functions."* Wargaming and what-if testing on an ongoing basis improve network resilience.

LET WHOLE-BUSINESS DATA PRIORITIES DETERMINE THE STRUCTURE AND FUNCTION OF YOUR NETWORKS

Digital resilience requires the commitment, coordination, and collaboration of the entire enterprise, top to bottom. Specific measures need to be taken to improve the resilience of your digital networks. The first step is to acquire a real-time picture of your network and all of its connections to the outside, as discussed in Chapter 6. Most companies have diagrams of their digital networks, but their network documentation is often years old. Networks change quickly as devices are added, taken away, or reconfigured, and virtual and cloud-based network segments appear, change, and vanish even more quickly. Moreover, a static map cannot adequately portray access across the network. Unless you can visualize your network accurately and in real-time, you cannot begin to take effective steps to improve its resilience.

You also need to verify that your devices are configured correctly. Devices often harbor default passwords and insecure services that any persistent attacker can and will discover—unless you discover them first. You need to determine whether any of your configurations violate your policies and standards, those of your industry, contractual obligations, or government regulations.

It is important to verify precisely all possible access to your networks and their data. This requires an end-to-end analysis, including a what-if analysis to determine the range of consequences of unauthorized access.

You want to know that your network is effectively segmented and that your security zones are correctly implemented according to whatever standards you adhere to. It is one thing to formulate prudent security policies, but these are of no value if they are not implemented and implemented properly. Making a network more resilient requires effective policies that are actually in force.

Identifying your highest-risk vulnerabilities and prioritizing them for patching enhances resilience. Prioritize risks by taking into account the nature of the vulnerability, the value of the asset, and how reachable that asset is. Vulnerabilities in hosts that are directly accessible to the Internet are of the highest priority, higher than those that are internal and inaccessible to the Internet. The thing is, you need to be able to *see* these high-priority problems before you can patch them. Patching based on the real risk of each vulnerability is a key part of increasing network resilience.

A network is useless if it fails to serve its users. But when a user requests a security change—for example, asking for access from this subnet to that subnet or from this port to that port—how do you know whether to approve the request? Does it violate policy? If it does, should you change policy? Conducting what-if analyses lets you ask the questions and get answers that show the effect of the proposed change. By visualizing the present state versus the future state of your network, you can make decisions that effectively balance efficiency and availability of access on the one hand against realistic security needs on the other.

Finally, making your network more resilient is also about accountability. You need to know that your network protects you as much as possible, and you need to be able to certify this to all stakeholders, from customers to regulators to board members. In-depth and timely visualization and scoring of your network enable you to make a business case for whatever changes—additional hardware, software, or services—are needed to enhance resilience.

MAKE THE BUSINESS CASE FOR DIGITAL RESILIENCE

Making a persuasive business case for network infrastructure that enhances resilience has always been hampered by a language barrier. "The arcane nature of cybersecurity makes it hard to engage effectively with the senior executive team. . . . Even those senior executives who feel they have a solid grasp of concepts like applications, data centers, networks, and desktop devices may throw up their hands in frustration when the discussion turns to access controls, machine learning to combat insider threats, and intrusion detection." Traditionally, "limitations in quantifying cybersecurity risks make it even harder to engage senior executives." Their principal frustration is the "lack of the type of meaningful metrics they use to assess productivity, quality, or risk in other areas." Executives who assess risk in extending credit, for example, have an array of scoring tools to aid making and justifying decisions. Risk officers in a variety of industries can turn to databases that report failures or injuries per so many thousands and often have well-established tables to demonstrate the impact of spending *x* dollars on reducing losses, failures, or injuries.

Employ software tools that quantify the resilience of the current network and data structures of the company and that allow for clear and objective what-if analysis of the impact of proposed changes in structure, access, hardware, and so on. Effective analytics enable objective comparison of the present state of the network with any number of future state scenarios, enabling nontechnical decision makers to evaluate the bang for their cybersecurity buck in increased resilience.[7]

The ability to quantify and prioritize resilience is important to allocating the resources necessary to protect your enterprise; however, making the business case for digital resilience should go beyond just defending against breaches and liabilities. Business is about adding value and selling the value you add. Resilience has value. Internally, the CISO (or equivalent) needs to demonstrate how what she proposes will add to the value chain and therefore enhance the value proposition offered to customers. Instead of making an entirely defensive case for engaging the enterprise in an initiative to enhance resilience, it is more effective to demonstrate the value of resilience as a benefit that can be promoted to customers. The resilience of your network and data-handling processes adds to the resilience of every customer network you engage with. Your resilience makes a positive impact on your customer's supply chain. Reliability, security, and confidence are strong selling points, especially when quantified by a score that is easy to compare to others. Increasing resilience should decrease the cost of protecting a network, because what is important in that network is now less vulnerable.

ACTION ITEM

Make a genuine business case for resilience with a persuasive cost-benefit analysis of specific security and resilience measures. Advocating for "security" and "resilience" as absolutes is both misleading and ineffective. Like any other business objective, security and resilience require investment. The case for making any investment must include a credible estimate of return on the proposed investment. Do not attempt to make this case in the language of information technology and cybersecurity. Speak the language of business.

Quantifying the impact of *x* dollars invested in strengthening a network by increasing digital resilience does more than answer a CEO's or board member's question about the cost of network security. It can become the basis of a positive, aggressive sales case for investing in resilience. If today's IT departments have increasingly become risk-management departments, it is high time that businesses promote the value *to their customers* of risk that is expertly and effectively managed. In an intensively networked business environment, how you manage your cyber-related risk will impact your customers and other partners either negatively or positively.

In the past, the most a digital security officer could hope to offer was an acceptable trade-off somewhere between optimum efficiency and optimum security. More recently, a CISO could make a persuasive argument that looking at the security/efficiency equation as a trade-off is a mistake. For the objective is not security as such, but managing risk in ways that allow the enterprise to more effectively realize opportunity.

Today, the CISO or his equivalent has an even better deal to offer the enterprise, namely the positive bottom-line impact of resilience as a value added to the company's products or services. Today's threat environment is a problem for you *and* for your customer. The quantifiable resilience you offer is, like any truly desirable merchandise, a solution to a problem, an answer to a question, and a response to a need.

THE RESILIENCE OF YOUR NETWORK ADDS VALUE TO THE NETWORKS WITH WHICH YOU CONNECT

I want to lead a profitable business. I also want my business to make the world a better place. I am convinced that building resilient networks requires that CISOs, CIOs, or their equivalents fully engage with the entire enterprise, from the board to the CEO to every employee who uses digital data, especially those in the frontline who deal with customers and clients. I have suggested that an important way for security leaders to integrate themselves and their operations into the whole business is to make a business case for resilience, not just defensively (although this is crucial) but also affirmatively, even aggressively. After all, creating resilience is not just something you *must do* to protect your business, it is also a positive contribution to the value chain, which adds value for customers, vendors, partners, and every entity who exchanges any information with your business. I claim that the certifiably resilient business has a competitive edge.

I want the competitive edge. But I also want to share my competitive edge with the business community because my business benefits even more from an environment populated by other resilient businesses. I want to collaborate with them to make them even more resilient, and I hope and expect that they want to collaborate with each other and with me in creating and sharing and reporting on best practices to increase the resilience of the networks that, in the end, we all share. To the degree that we can make the current digital ecosystem healthier, we all win—and by "we," I mean businesses, institutions, governments, consumers, and every entity that is interconnected through the Internet. In other words, all of us.

ACTION ITEM

Do well by doing good. Investing in digital resilience benefits your enterprise and the networks it directly controls, even as it makes the business community—the digital ecosystem—healthier. Think of enhancing your resilience as safeguarding not only your "personal" health but "public" health, the well-being of your community. As the health of each individual benefits from the health of the community, so the resilience of each enterprise benefits from the overall resilience of the digital ecosystem.

Knowing your own network and how it connects to the networks beyond it is the first step toward making your network more resilient. Make your network more resilient, and you have not only taken a step toward protecting yourself and your business, you have increased the health of the digital ecosystem, thus improving the health of all. But it is in your interest to reach beyond your network as well.

Digital commerce websites continue to proliferate through every business. Unquestionably, these create greater opportunities for businesses as well as consumers. Unquestionably, too, they create greater opportunities for cybercriminals—as well as for the overtime operation of Murphy's Law. As more and more businesses become more and more dependent on the Internet, networks become increasingly likely to break down due to nefarious activity and to human error caused by increasing complexity.

Resilient businesses put in place systems and other measures to work around failures, and they seek to prevent those failures in the first place by requiring more stringent quality of service (QoS) guarantees from their ISPs. This adds costs, and it may run afoul of current or future net neutrality regulations.[8] Ultimately, the resilience of any business depends on the resilience of the Internet infrastructure. Who will pay for the necessary investment to ensure that the Internet serves the ever-growing need for capacity and "smart" delivery? The business community needs to unite to answer this and other questions.

TREAT "THE CLOUD" AS PART OF YOUR NETWORK—BECAUSE IT IS

For some years now, companies have been migrating their data centers to the cloud. As early as 2011, a McKinsey study found that 85 percent of large companies interviewed reported that cloud computing was one of their top innovation priorities, and 70 percent said that they were either planning or had already launched a "private cloud" program.[9] Whereas the "public cloud" is open to all users and is predominantly self-managed by the users, the "private cloud" offers "standardized . . . virtualized, and highly automated environments to host [the] business applications" of tenant companies.[10] Private-cloud hosting is a "single-tenant" environment; that is, hardware, storage, and network are dedicated to a single company.

Back in 2012, the authors of *Trillions* criticized the very term "cloud" because, like "cyberspace," it evokes a vision of ubiquity, eternity, and changeless stability. They suggested that "*Hindenburg*" was a more accurate description than "cloud" because many storage and hosting operations exhibited "remarkable . . . fragility." Clouds? They were "corporate cloud-balloons," which, like "the infamous exploding zeppelin," look substantial but are "really . . . very delicate," inherently insecure, built on an "architecture that is vulnerable to assault" and subject as well to the vicissitudes of corporate takeovers and "plain old changes in business strategy."[11]

The private cloud has addressed many of these public cloud vulnerabilities and arguably enhances the security of data and hosting operations by allowing hardware, data storage, and networking provisions to be designed to high standards that are inaccessible to others who use the same data center. Moreover, whereas the public cloud cannot deliver such government- and industry-mandated compliance as Sarbanes Oxley, PCI DSS (Payment Card Industry Data Security Standard), and HIPAA (Health Insurance Portability and Accountability Act), the costlier but still cost-effective private cloud can.

It is tempting to see migration to the cloud as migration away from the need for network resilience. It is not. Rather, the cloud is a data storage and hosting node that becomes part of your network. Indeed, today, the digital infrastructures for nearly all Global 2000 companies include not only on-premises and cloud networks, but also software-defined virtualized networks. These are part of the new dynamic digital geography, and just because the networks that result from their cloud and virtualized components are large, complex, and constantly changing does not mean that enterprise stakeholders can simply ignore them. They are part of the network, and the entire network must be assessed.

ACTION ITEMS

Whether you use the public cloud, the private cloud, or both, you need to ask questions of your vendor:

- Ask about the *physical, real-world* security of your data. Where is the vendor's data center located? (Hint: At the foot of Vesuvius is not good.)
- Ask what certifications the cloud vendor can produce. (SSAE 16 certification is widely regarded as the gold standard, and the Cloud Security Alliance [CSA] offers relevant certifications as well.[12])
- Ask the vendor what happens in the case of data loss. (This should be clearly covered in the provider's Service Level Agreement, or SLA.) Any reputable cloud service provider will provide you with a downtime history so you can judge its reliability for yourself.
- Understand how virtual network segments connect with the physical segments, and understand how this impacts security and resilience.

"INFORMATION SECURITY THREATS ARE SET TO WORSEN": WHAT TO DO ABOUT IT

Although an intelligently acquired and managed private cloud may increase the digital resilience of your business while also lowering costs, it is not a desert island remote from all threats, and it is still wired into the Internet infrastructure we all share. The Information Security Forum (ISF), an independent, not-for-profit business-oriented organization "dedicated to investigating, clarifying, and resolving key issues in information security and risk management," annually publishes *Threat Horizon,* a report that examines a two-year window to provide a "forward-looking view of increasing threats." *Threat Horizon 2018* is subtitled "Lost in a maze of uncertainty," and if that doesn't sound comforting, well, the coming environment does not promise to be a comfortable one.[13]

"Information security threats are set to worsen," the report begins. "Organizations risk becoming disoriented and losing their way in a maze of uncertainty, as they grapple with complex technology, proliferation of data, increased regulation, and a debilitating skills shortage." As repeatedly suggested in this book, acquiring a comprehensive, comprehensible, timely model of your full network is the first step toward gaining or recovering your orientation so that you can make it through the maze. But while such a model is essential, it is not sufficient in a threat environment expanded by universal technology adoption. The ISF forecasts that the among the threats that will dominate 2018 are leaks of sensitive information through the Internet of Things, increasing reliance on opaque algorithms that compromise the integrity of companies by reducing transparency, and increasing incidence of rogue governments using terrorist groups to launch cyberattacks.[14]

Just as creating digital resilience requires embracing the entire business, not just the digital networks themselves, so the emerging digital threats go beyond the mechanics of network attacks. *Threat Horizon 2018* predicts that "unmet board expectations [will be] exposed by a major incident," demonstrating that the security expectations of boards of directors "will quickly accelerate beyond their information security functions' ability to deliver."[15] This prediction underscores the imperative to make digital resilience a whole-business objective. Organizations cannot afford a disconnect between the technologists and a nontechnical C-suite and board.

The urgency of integrating digital resilience across the entire business will be amplified even more if another ISF prediction proves valid, namely the withdrawal of many insurers from the still-developing cyber insurance market.[16] With insurance options reduced, companies will be cornered, finding themselves with no viable means for transferring their cyber risk. (The most conscientiously innovative businesses never want to abandon clients in need or a vital market. Right now, however, insurance companies have no reliable way to evaluate cyber risk comprehensively, and so their coverage is limited and by no means cheap. Several security firms work with insurance providers to create viable metrics to help them make more meaningful actuarial assessments based on the analysis of the particular enterprise and network that are being insured. Evaluation of the threat environment (the outside in) *and* the network (the inside out) is required. As mentioned in Chapter 6, RedSeal evaluates the network and can assist in understanding the degree of an outside threat.

Finally, ISF predicts friction between digital businesses and governments, thereby provoking governments to increase regulation. "Aggressive commercial strategies (by companies disrupting their sector) will prompt politicians and regulators to look at the domestic, commercial, and security impacts of new technologies." In particular, ISF expects that "regulatory and legislative changes will impose new restrictions on how personal data is handled," thereby delaying the deployment of innovative cloud services "without necessarily achieving the desired improvements to data protection."[17]

The coming friction between business and government regulators may be especially destructive because the only way to improve the resilience of our digital ecosystem is through a productive partnership among all Internet stakeholders *and* governments. *Threat Horizon 2018* predicts that the "technical capabilities of cybercriminals will surpass those of organizations," thereby expanding "gaps in international policing" and exposing companies to greater impact from cyberattacks.[18]

RESILIENCE AND SOCIAL RESPONSIBILITY: WHERE COMPETITION ENDS

"Some of the issues related to cybersecurity can be highly emotional and politicized," the authors of *Beyond Cybersecurity* correctly observe. This had led to "significant disagreements"—many of them ideologically rather than operationally based—"about how to proceed in the areas of collaboration and policy development." While "almost everyone agrees that companies should share intelligence about attacks more extensively," there is great disagreement over whether this sharing can take place under existing legal regimes or only if the government intervenes to provide legal immunity to companies that share. In addition, while some CISOs suggest that "the public sector could play a valuable role in setting and funding a research agenda" to improve the security and resilience of network and Internet infrastructure, others argue "that governments could not set intelligent research priorities in as dynamic a space as cybersecurity." This disagreement goes to a fundamental conflict among CISOs about government regulation. Whereas 40 percent of technology executives interviewed by the *Beyond Cybersecurity* authors said "that, on balance, cybersecurity regulation encouraged companies to be more secure in a helpful way," 46 percent protested that government regulation either requires "a lot of time and effort but does not make companies more secure, or that it actively makes companies less secure." The leading complaint was that "regulations were cumbersome and locked into place outdated practices." Moreover, regulators often "lacked the expertise to make the right judgments about cybersecurity practices."[19] One answer may be more thoughtful and consistent enforcement of existing regulations.

Debate is a good thing, provided it does not result in paralysis. Businesses must recognize that the Internet is a critical infrastructure for any developed nation and, of course, for the world. In the United States, the power grid has long been owned chiefly by the private sector yet recognized as a strategic infrastructure that has been subject to federal legislation and regulation. It seems to me incontrovertible that formulating a national cybersecurity strategy encompassing the Internet and its infrastructures is essential to the survival and prosperity of any nation, including the United States.

Creating the strategy will require legislation and regulation; however, governments must recognize that the resilience of the Internet depends in large part on its agility, its ability to expand and adapt quickly and to incorporate new technologies rapidly. In short, governments must recognize that the most intensive users of the Internet, namely the members of the business community, have the greatest stake in its security and are best positioned for the most granular understanding of what is required to continuously increase its resilience—to make it both more secure *and* more productive. Governments must further recognize that the processes of legislation and regulation, which are (and should be) deliberate, cannot keep pace with networked digital technology. Based on an acknowledgment by business of the necessity of a national cybersecurity strategy and an acknowledgment by government that business is best positioned to shape the resilience of the strategy's core element, the Internet, the only viable partnership for the creation, maintenance, and continuous improvement of Internet resilience is a genuine partnership of government and business.

In equal partnership with business, each developed nation needs to formulate a national cybersecurity strategy. Each of these strategies must be shared with all nations, each nation assisting others with best practices. The most desirable objective, finally, may be a set of internationally agreed norms relating to the use and management of the Internet. A formal and restrictive international cybersecurity convention administered by the United Nations or other international body may be desirable to promote and ensure Internet resilience.

But there is reason to be skeptical. The closest thing we have to a comprehensive international convention on Internet security or resilience is the Convention on Cybercrime, which the Council of Europe (COE) opened for signature on November 23, 2001, and which entered into force on July 1, 2004. As of December 2016, fifty states have ratified the convention and are party to it (and another five have signed, but not yet ratified, it).[20] The convention establishes "a common criminal policy aimed at the protection of society against cybercrime."[21] Laudable as this purpose is, the convention places requirements on signatories that demand a significant compromise of traditional national sovereignty. For instance, signatories are required to "adopt legislation banning various computer crimes, including illegal access and interception, data and system interference, misuse of devices, forgery, fraud, child pornography, and intellectual property offenses." They must also "adopt laws concerning the investigation of computer-related crimes" and must agree to "cooperate in the investigation and prosecution of such crimes with other countries (i.e., via extradition and mutual law-enforcement assistance)."[22]

In response to such requirements, signatories created "'consensus' on computer crimes only by adopting vague definitions that are subject to different interpretations by different states. Even with vague definitions, many nations conditioned their consent on declarations and reservations (the United States had more than a half dozen) that further diluted the scope of covered crimes, making the treaty's obligations even less uniform and less demanding." The lesson of the Cybercrime Convention is that "nations significantly disagree about what digital practices should be outlawed and are deeply skeptical about even the weakest forms of international cooperation in this area. It is a cautionary tale for those who believe in the feasibility of a broader cybersecurity treaty involving more nations and covering more ambitious topics that bear a closer relationship to sovereignty and national security."[23]

If we adopt the skeptical view, which I believe is a healthy option, we are left with developing a more collegial relationship between national governments and businesses, international regulatory bodies and businesses, nations and other nations, and businesses and other businesses. Given the fluid nature of the global Internet, the collegial approach may be the most effective, and its objective should be the evolving formulation of norms to promote and protect the productive, peaceful, most secure yet freest use of the global Internet possible. Creating strategies based on the direct and inclusive collaboration among governments, businesses, and individuals—all as stakeholders in the global Internet—provides the most promising prospect for achieving a level of digital resilience that reflects the most resilient networks found in nature and history.

TAKEAWAY

Digital infrastructure and operations must be addressed as issues that impact the entire enterprise, and digital resilience must be treated as a business value. Increasingly, IT professionals are being given what businesses urgently need to give them: a seat in the C-suite and on the board. Nevertheless, the current state of cybersecurity too often delivers both inadequate security *and* security that hobbles innovation and agility. Business leaders must acknowledge that cybersecurity alone is insufficient to manage digital risk. The time has come to go beyond cybersecurity by working toward digital resilience. Fortunately, today's CISOs and their equivalent are positioned to promote the positive bottom-line impact of resilience as a value added to the company's products or services. In addition, investing in digital resilience benefits the entire business community by making the digital ecosystem healthier. Looking to the future, it is apparent that formulating a national cybersecurity strategy encompassing the Internet and its infrastructures will be increasingly essential to the survival and prosperity of any nation, including the United States. Doubtless, this will require legislation and regulation; however, governments must recognize that the resilience of the global Internet depends on its agility, its ability to expand and adapt quickly. Governments must therefore recognize that the most intensive users of the Internet, namely the members of the business community, have the greatest stake in its well-being and are best positioned for the most granular understanding of what is required to continuously increase its resilience.

8

ACHIEVING DIGITAL RESILIENCE

A Top-Down Guide

Organizational relationships, priorities, and risks change over time. They change because of new leadership, external factors affecting the business, new recruits with new ideas, and evolving supply chain and customer relationships. Cybersecurity and its implementation are among the forces of change that impact organizations.

By the early 1970s, arguments over the pros and cons of innovative "flat" corporate organizations versus traditional hierarchical, or "tall," organizations were shading distinctly toward the flat end of the spectrum. More and more C-suite executives and boards of directors were being drawn to the idea of elevating employee levels of responsibility, streamlining management layers, improving the coordination and speed of communication among employees, facilitating decision making, and—not least of all—reducing or eliminating middle-management salaries. Besides these business considerations, flattening out corporate hierarchies seemed a desirable affirmation of democratic values. Flat felt good.[1] The status quo, represented in the "super bureaucracies" of the 1920s, became the new status quo of the flat organization by the 1970s. From here, by the early twenty-first century, the flat model spawned such ideas as eco-leadership, collaborative leadership, and distributed leadership. These are what business journalist Vivian Giang calls the "super flat" organizational model.[2]

"When we look at organizations that are flatter, there's both top-down and bottom-up decision making," MIT professor of management and organizational studies Deborah Ancona told Giang. Ancona pointed out that "a lot more tasks are given to people lower down in the organization. There's more empowerment and freedom given to people." In effect, as Giang observes, in today's super-flat organizations, "everyone needs to step up and be the leader."[3]

LIABILITY IN TODAY'S "SUPER FLAT" ORGANIZATIONS: WHY RESILIENCE IS MORE IMPORTANT THAN EVER

At least some of the democratic idealism that clings to the super-flat organization may be aspirational hype, but it is almost certainly true that even large corporate structures have never been flatter. This is in large part a function of digital networking within the organization, among different organizations, and among people inside and outside any organization. In the old analog days, the top-level executives not only made most of the money, they possessed most of the data—the information necessary to make key decisions and run the company. Today, thanks to intranets and the Internet, *almost* everyone in a business has access to *almost* all data.

Where tall analog organizations imposed draconian restrictions on who could connect to whom, both within the company and outside of it, today's substantially flatter organizations promote connection pretty much at will. The ability for anyone in a company to have a personal email conversation with the CEO has cemented this change to flat.

This is efficient, productive, and good—mostly. But while each connection enhances transparency and presents business opportunities, it also poses business risks. And that is when the realization hits CEOs and boards of directors that while leadership may be widely distributed across their enterprise, liability for the corporation is ultimately concentrated at the top of even the flattest of modern organizations. In managing this twenty-first-century flat, digital, transparent corporation, resilience is more important than ever. We must be prepared for more risks, more disruptions, and the creation and dissemination of more misinformation.

The 2013 breach of Target Corporation (Chapter 1) not only compromised the personally identifiable information of some 70 million people (nearly 30 percent of the adult population of the United States), but resulted in the outright digital theft of 40 million credit cards and cost Target in excess of a quarter-billion dollars.[4] The breach also brought a barrage of lawsuits against the company by the banks that issued the affected credit cards, by shareholders, and by customers. Target's CEO was fired, and directors and officers were "caught in the crossfire" of "a series of derivative lawsuits," in which "shareholders claimed that the retailer's board and C-suite violated their fiduciary duties by not providing proper oversight for the company's information security program, not making prompt and accurate public disclosures about the breach, and ignoring red flags that Target's IT systems were vulnerable to attack."[5] The four derivative suits filed in federal court were subsequently consolidated and eventually dismissed, but only after nearly two years of costly inquiry and investigation. In the end, an independent oversight committee did recommend replacing the board.[6]

The 2013 Target case and its fallout were a wakeup call to boards and the occupants of the C-suite. Today, everybody must assume a degree of leadership, but leadership toward digital resilience must ultimately be a top-down initiative. If protecting digital data assets were strictly a matter of cybersecurity, top executives and board members could turn everything over to a CISO (Chief Information Security Officer) or a CIO (Chief Information Officer) and audit their work on a quarterly or yearly basis. But as we have demonstrated in this book, cybersecurity implemented by itself is not likely to fail, it is certain to fail. A recent article in *The Economist* documented this fact alarmingly. The blunt title of the piece is telling: “Why Everything Is Hackable.” The second paragraph catalogs some of the biggest cyber hits of 2016: $81 million lifted from the central bank of Bangladesh, the theft and subsequent leaking of CIA data and NSA hacking tools, the paralyzing distributed denial of service attack against Internet performance management company Dyn via the Internet of Things, and, of course, the hacking of the Democratic National Committee’s email servers, the WikiLeaks data dumps that followed, and the creation of a cloud of uncertainty over the U.S. presidential election and the presidency it produced. But the hacks, the exploits, and the crimes are not the focus of the article. The victims’ vulnerability is—and that vulnerability, it turns out, is universal: “everything is hackable.”[7]

We could say that businesses face a clear and present danger, but the more salient truth is that boards and C-suite leaders face a clear and present certainty since they bear the liability for failure. As the 2013 Target breach demonstrated, cybercrime is a global criminal enterprise that in many astounding ways is run like the businesses it attacks. "Obscure forums oil the trade in stolen credit-card details, sold in batches of thousands at a time. Data-dealers hawk 'exploits': flaws in code that allow malicious attackers to subvert systems. You can also buy 'ransomware,' with which to encrypt photos and documents on victims' computers before charging them for the key that will unscramble the data." The traditional pop-culture view of hackers as rogue savants supremely skilled in the black arts of malicious coding—and therefore, like the Leonardo da Vincis of the world, few and far between—is dead. So much malware is commercially available through online vendors "that coding skills are now entirely optional." It makes cybercrime easier, a lot less risky, and great deal more profitable than buying a gun and walking into the neighborhood store to rob it. Even botnets—"flocks of compromised computers created by software like [the IoT-oriented] Mirai, which can then be used to flood websites with traffic, knocking them offline until a ransom is paid—can be rented by the hour." What is more, "Just like a legitimate business, the bot-herders will, for a few dollars extra, provide technical support if anything goes wrong."[8]

CYBERCRIMINALS ARE NOT JUST CRIMINALS, THEY ARE YOUR COMPETITION

Caleb Barlow, president of IBM Security, cites a United Nations report estimating that 80 percent of all attacks are conducted by "highly organized and ultra-sophisticated criminal gangs"—New Age thugs, I like to say. Barlow points out that this 80 percent "represents one of the largest illegal economies in the world, topping out at, now get this, $445 billion," which is "larger than the GDP of 160 nations, including Ireland, Finland, Denmark, and Portugal, to name a few."[9]

The cybercriminals the UN report is talking about resemble the attacker that hit Target in 2013. They "operate like highly regimented, legitimate businesses. Their employees work Monday through Friday. They take the weekends off. How do we know this? We know this because our security researchers see repeated spikes of malware on a Friday afternoon. The bad guys, after a long weekend with the wife and kids, come back in to see how well things went." Via the so-called Dark Web, they offer "everything . . . from a base-level attack to a much more advanced version. In fact, in many cases, you even see gold, silver, and bronze levels of service. You can check references. You can even buy attacks that come with a money-back guarantee if you're not successful." In fact, these criminal enterprises "look like an Amazon or an eBay. You see products, prices, ratings, and reviews. Of course, if you're going to buy an attack, you're going to buy from a reputable criminal with good ratings, right?"[10]

Cybercrime has evolved into a viable business, with a remarkably low bar to entry. Legitimate businesses suddenly find themselves facing a whole new category of competition. No CEO and no board of directors would even think of failing to address their company's competition or other "legitimate" threats. No C-level executive or board member would disclaim responsibility for dealing with the emergence of a new category of competitor by declaring it a problem for the chief marketing officer or the director of sales. No, it is no longer an option for C-suites and boards to view cyber threats and cyber vulnerabilities as matters for IT or the CIO or the CISO. These are whole-business issues that demand solutions starting at the top.

In truth, criminal cyber enterprises are not just competitors, they are super-competitors. Not because they are geniuses—they are not—but because the very nature of today's rapidly evolving

Internet creates new business vulnerabilities for every astounding business opportunity it enables. *The Economist* is a journal that likes to quantify what it prints. In the case of "all this hacking," however, *The Economist* throws up its editorial hands, calling the cost of cybercrime "anyone's guess." Nevertheless, "all agree it is likely to rise, because the scope for malice is about to expand remarkably." The expansion is due to the fact that, as security analyst Bruce Schneier puts it, "We are building a world-sized robot." This is the IoT, the networked computerization of "everything from cars and electricity meters to children's toys, medical devices, and light bulbs."[11]

Just about every electrically powered device in our world is being designed to connect with the Internet, which means that just about anything can, does, or soon will connect to the networks we think of as "our own" and "under our control." Traditional cybersecurity—the kind that was once the exclusive responsibility of IT, the CIO, or the CISO—is all about defending network perimeters. Much as insurgent wars—such as Vietnam during the 1960s and 1970s—forced traditional militaries to transform themselves into organizations capable of fighting armed conflicts that no longer had a defined "front," so the IoT is forcing businesses to discard the very notion of any network "perimeter" to defend. "The default assumption," University of Cambridge computer scientist Robert Watson says, "is that everything is vulnerable."[12]

ACTION ITEMS

Writers of memos and directives love the heading *Action Items*. But what action items are appropriate when *everything* is vulnerable? Big companies are turning "to an old remedy for such unavoidable risks: insurance," the current market for which has been reported at $3 billion to $4 billion a year, with 60 percent annual growth.[13] The risk of cyberattack is indeed "unavoidable," and insurance is a prudent tool for managing unavoidable risk, but, like cybersecurity itself, though necessary, it is not sufficient.

Faced with unavoidable risks, corporate leadership has three choices:

1. Get off the Internet. (In other words, go out of business.)
2. Insure the enterprise for losses at quite possibly unrealistic or at least unsustainable levels.
3. Take steps to achieve digital resilience—not with the impossible objective of avoiding the risk of cyberattack, but of managing cyberattack, dodging or defeating intrusion where possible, containing and thereby neutralizing a breach when it occurs, preventing (or at least minimizing) exfiltration, and learning from the incident to improve resilience while, in the meantime, continuing to do business even while under attack and, when damage occurs, recovering as quickly and completely as possible.

As we have seen, digital resilience is not a product one can simply purchase and deploy. It is a state of mind and operational philosophy that, in due course, is destined to be embedded in all future management training, schooling, and corporations. Why "destined"? Because only organizations that embed resilience will have a future. Although resilience, like quality control and quality assurance, can at first seem like just another additional expense, the fact is that, once implemented, resilience becomes a competitive advantage—truly a whole-business issue.

Action Item #1

Create awareness at the highest levels of the enterprise—the C-suite and the boardroom—of both the risks associated with your digital infrastructure and the certainty of cyberattack and its potential impact.

Action Item #2

Accept and understand that cyber insurance, while prudent and necessary, is not sufficient to mitigate the unavoidable risk of cyberattack. For one thing, currently available insurance does not begin to cover all costs associated with a breach. For another, insurers have yet to deploy technology and methodology to properly measure the risk they are being asked to cover. Most providers focus more-or-less exclusively on the threat environment and do not measure an organization's ability to defend itself, which is a critical component in evaluating risk and rationally determining the scope and pricing of coverage. Policies, moreover, usually cover only out-of-pocket costs associated with notifications and other statutory reporting and compliance. By contrast, if the factory burns to the ground, insurance will rebuild it, pay lost wages of workers, cover inventory, and, in some cases, even cover lost revenues. Cyber insurance adheres to no such model of coverage. Suppose, for example, that you need to replace all the routers in your organization because a systemic digital flaw was discovered. Cyber insurance does not cover this expense. And that expense could be very considerable if you had to replace, say, 10,000 routers—the number in a not-very-large business. In any case, corporate leadership cannot blithely hand off management of cyber risk to a Chief Risk Officer (CRO). It is a business issue that demands whole-business involvement led from the top.

Action Item #3

Accept and understand that perimeter and detection cybersecurity is necessary but not sufficient to protect the digital data assets of the company, its customers, its suppliers and vendors, and other stakeholders. The assumption throughout the C-suite and the board must be that everything is vulnerable, including internal assets; therefore, to enable the organization's survival, cybersecurity must be paired with digital resilience—the ability to respond to, counteract, and contain the event.

Action Item #4

Through audit, find out if your company is as digitally secure as it can be. Boards need to audit cybersecurity regularly. Yet this action item is something of a trick because you already possess the answer to the question *Are we optimally secured against attack?* It is, *No, we are* not *optimally secured against attack.*

Why not? *Because no company can both be digitally connected to the world* and *optimally secured against a successful attack.* Former FBI director Robert S. Mueller III said back in 2012, "I am convinced that there are only two types of companies: those that have been hacked and those that will be. And even they are converging into one category: companies that have been hacked and will be hacked again."[14] No cybersecurity solution is bulletproof. Cyberattack is both frequent and inevitable. Given sufficient time, *successful* cyberattack—an attack that penetrates your security and impacts your business—is also inevitable. It's what you know and how you respond that makes the most difference in how you emerge from an attack.

Action Item #5

Determine your risk appetite. Top leadership needs to ask and answer four key questions:

1. What risks can we control?
2. What risks must we accept because we cannot control them?
3. In balancing exposure to attack with the business opportunities presented by openness of digital access, how much risk are we prepared to stomach?
4. What can we do to manage and mitigate the risk we decide to accept?

These questions are not unique to digital resilience. They are already asked regarding practices and policies throughout many other aspects of the business. Often, organizations have risk officers who assess risks based on the type of business they're in. The cyber thugs want your data. They want to steal it, sell it, disrupt your operations, or wreak havoc on you and others. How your business acquires the data—what you do for a living—is of no concern to them. If you are big, have data, or have access to others who have the data and control, you are a target. Since data is the target, senior management *must* lead the effort to protect that data, whether you are making bread or making steel.

Action Item #6

Understand the difference between digital security *and* digital resilience. You don't need to reread this book. Here's the nutshell: *Security* is about locking up and hunkering down. *Resilience* is about standing up to do business while fighting back.

Although leadership must demand the best digital security compatible with doing business in an intensively connected digital ecosystem, there is a danger that a CISO or CIO is in the position of the proverbial person armed only with a hammer and to whom, therefore, the entire world looks like a nail. Security is a *security* issue, whereas resilience is a *business* issue, and that is why it is incumbent upon top leadership—the CEO and the board—to ensure that the enterprise has the best and most appropriate digital security *compatible with doing business optimally.*

Digital security proposes to keep attackers out of your network mainly by defending the network perimeter using antimalware detection software and firewalls. The problem is that no perimeter defense that is compatible with connectivity—in other words, compatible with doing business—is bulletproof. If you connect intensively enough to do business optimally, you expose your internal network to attacks, some of which will penetrate your perimeter defenses. Besides, today's cyber threats come from the inside as well as the outside. So, one way or another, an attacker *will* get into your network. That is why your enterprise must achieve digital resilience.

Action Item #7

Lead your company toward resilience. "A computer at its basic level has an engine that runs things and a list called 'memory' from which it fetches instructions on what to do next," Dr. Phyllis A. Schneck, President Obama's DHS deputy undersecretary for cybersecurity and communications, explained in her keynote address to the 2016 NACD Global Summit. "A hack is simply: I've got your next instruction, and I can make your computer do what I want it to do. And once I do that once, I can do it forever, because I'm in." Assume that your network will be penetrated; therefore, start leading your company toward resilience. It is a capability and a strategy that will give you the "ability to fight while under attack and stay alive"—that is, stay connected, doing business.[15]

Action Item #8

Frame resilience as a business issue, not as a security issue. Old habits die hard. Make an affirmative effort to avoid misfiling *resilience* under *security.* Treat it as you would any other business issue that involves and impacts the whole enterprise. This means planning for and budgeting resilience not as an operational adjunct, a regulatory burden, or so much defensive "hardware," but as a positive business asset. Make it a competitive weapon. Not only will resilience help you to prevent data exfiltration, minimizing damage while enabling you to continue doing business, it will facilitate recovery from the most successful attacks. Beyond these benefits to the enterprise, resilience, properly promoted from the top, will attract customers, partners, and investors, all of whom are becoming increasingly savvy when choosing vendors, partners, and investments.

Sixty-eight percent of responders to EY's Nineteenth Global Information Security Survey 2016–17 "would not increase their information security spending even if a supplier was attacked—even though a supplier is a direct route for an attacker into the organization."[16] On the one hand, this indicates a stunning failure to appreciate the stark fact that the security of your network is only as strong as the security of the networks with which you connect; on the other hand, however, it suggests that nearly a third of corporate leaders *do* value the security of the digital networks operated by their vendors and other partners. By treating your network's resilience as an asset to the whole business, the board and the C-suite are positioned to promote a corporate culture of resilience as a value to customers, suppliers, investors, and other stakeholders. Perhaps "only" a third of business leaders currently recognize this value. Your promotion of resilience, from the top down, can be instrumental in growing that number by educating your customers and others in the value resilient digital practices offers the entire business community. Increasingly, consumers and businesses can be expected to choose to work with organizations that have demonstrably robust resilience policies and platforms.

Action Item #9

Secure a whole-business commitment. The board and CEO must be united in getting all C-suite and department and other executives not only committed to, but actively involved in, creating and maintaining digital resilience. This commitment and involvement requires the actions that follow in items #10 and #11.

Action Item #10

Adopt resilient measures that address the whole network with the objective of protecting data rather than protecting individual hardware devices. Recruit the entire organization to contribute the detailed working knowledge and insight required to prioritize all data assets according to the business value of data items as well as their accessibility to attack. Assets of greater business value require more access controls than items of lesser business value; however, items of greater business value that are not readily accessible from outside of the network may require fewer access controls than assets of lesser value that exist on parts of the network readily accessible to the outside. Thus, prioritizing data assets requires a two-factor analysis that is both a strategic business assessment and a technical assessment. Top leadership should require this assessment from those best positioned to perform it. Creating a truly resilient digital strategy—one that balances the security of selective user privilege against scope of access—requires the diverse insights of the entire organization. The goal is to provide efficiently differentiated protection for the company's data. Critically important assets call for close control of access as well as high levels of encryption. Less sensitive data assets can be made more widely and readily accessible.

Action Item #11

Prioritize your assets, and, at regular intervals, audit the measures established in Action Item #10. The board of directors should not micromanage data asset prioritization. Nevertheless, it must accept responsibility for regularly auditing prioritization. It also should, when necessary, question the rationality of the priorities with an eye toward ensuring that data resilience throughout the enterprise is based on a productive and prudent balance between accessibility and security.

Action Item #12

Nurture a resilient organizational culture from the top down. Because it is both key to the survival of the enterprise as well as a feature of its value proposition, digital resilience must become an integral aspect of the culture of the organization. In a society, culture tends to develop from the bottom up, but in a business, culture emanates from the top, through the leadership of the board and the CEO and, from there, throughout the C-suite, through operational executives, and down to the frontline employees. This said, the entire organization needs to buy into the values and standards of the culture, which means that everyone must be involved in integrating digital resilience throughout the enterprise. Data is accorded lofty status in a resilient organization. Employees at every level should be recruited and trained to value and protect whatever data assets they handle. Nowhere is this more important than among personnel who deal with customer data and other core, critical assets of an organization.

Action Item #13

Take basic training for digital hygiene. Top leadership, including board members, should receive the same instruction in basic safe computing practices that all employees receive. "Social engineering"—the cons and deceptions at the core of pretexting, phishing, and other exploits—is the most common means by which attackers gain access to a network, and sophisticated attackers make a special effort to target high-ranking executives on the assumption that they have access to more of the most valuable information. The 2013 Target breach and the 2015–2016 breach of the Democratic National Committee, cybercrimes of historic proportion and consequence, began with social engineering—deceiving some human being to click on an email-borne link that deployed a piece of malware onto a computer system and therefore throughout the network. Awareness of social engineering exploits and how to avoid them should be universal throughout the organization. An attacker needs just one door to open. Whether that door belongs to the chairman of the board or to an intern matters surprisingly little.

Action Item #14

Deploy resilience in all business processes. Resilience is best applied to processes rather than divisions or functions or departments or individuals. Boards and the C-suite should require that resilience be designed into such processes as product development, marketing, sales, human resources, and the supply chain. In planning, overseeing, and auditing resilience, top leadership should think in terms of processes instead of organizational silos. At bottom, most business activities consist of a network of connected processes. Building into all business processes such features as strategic redundancy, alternative sequences, and segmentation of operations is a resilient approach to workflows that enable businesses to survive attacks and buy time to contain breaches while continuing to do business. This may be the easiest of all actions to take.

Action Item #15

Know your network and digital assets. Forty-nine percent of businesses responding to EY's Nineteenth Global Information Security Survey 2016–17 "doubt that they are going to be able to continue to identify suspicious traffic over their networks." Little wonder, since 46 percent "are also concerned about their ability to know all their [hardware] assets, . . . how they are going to keep these devices bug free (43 percent), how they will be able to patch vulnerabilities fast enough (43 percent), and about their abilities to manage the growth in access points to their organization (35 percent)."[17] If we average these results, we can assume conservatively that four out of ten companies effectively admit to not *knowing* their networks. In consequence, even if they can find vulnerabilities, these companies (and, truth be told, probably many more) have little or no idea how accessible those vulnerabilities are to an attacker. Nor do they know what vulnerabilities lurk in unknown portions of their network. Moreover, they do not fully understand how making a change in one place (such as adding a device or changing a user privilege) affects the network as a whole, perhaps changing the status of its exposure.

Digital resilience begins with knowledge, not as a static map of your networks and their connections to the outside, but as a close to real-time picture of the network. Software tools are available to provide this dynamic picture. Without such timely knowledge, no organization can achieve digital resilience.

Action Item #16

Create a common language using a common metric to talk about risk, security, and resilience. A picture, even one that refreshes frequently to reflect the changing realities of your networks, their devices, and their connections to the outside, may not be universally intelligible, especially to nontechnical specialists from your board and C-suite. Fortunately, digital resilience can be measured; therefore, measure it. Better yet, *score* your networks in terms of digital resilience, expressing quantitatively both their resilience and their level of vulnerability with high objectivity and low ambiguity. This will enable CISOs and CIOs to make their *business* case to the CEO and the board to justify investment in specific aspects of the company's digital infrastructure, or reallocate their precious capital and human talent to mitigate risk in the most accessible parts of the network. Armed with a resilience score, top leadership has a guide that enables cost-effective allocation of digital devices and software resources to strategically enhance high-performing resilience.

Action Item #17

Ask—What if? This is the magic of resilience. Using your network mapping and resilience scoring tools, test a variety of what-if scenarios to calculate the impact of proposed changes in the network—addition or deletion of connections, alterations in access privileges, addition or removal of devices. The Pentagon has looked at the world for decades, asking what if about an array of potential enemies. The same concept can be applied to resilience in a business. Score how such changes will enhance connectivity (and therefore business opportunity) versus how the changes will pose security risks or reduce business opportunity. Test the effect of changes before the changes are made. The resulting scores should be expressed in terms meaningful to nontechnical board members and C-suite officers.

Action Item #18

Understand the digital ecosystem by evaluating your connections. In December 2016, hackers impersonating a recording company executive sent emails to a music management company and to a management and recording company that persuaded human beings at both firms to send them Lady Gaga's stem files, the files recording engineers and producers use to remix and remaster records. "The heist," *The New York Times* reported, "was a classic example of how hackers exploit the weakest link in the extensive chain of vendors, postproduction studios and collaborators that corporations must trust with their most valuable intellectual property."[18]

The thing is, your network ceases to be exclusively yours the instant you connect to another network. Whether you are Lady Gaga or Target Corporation, a breach is enabled by vulnerabilities in your network, but it may begin with a breach in the network of a vendor—in the case of Target, a certified vendor—who has privileged access to your network. In the Target case, neither the vendor nor Target detected the insecurity. Nevertheless, the vendor's malware issue became Target's problem when the two networks communicated.[19] As for Lady Gaga, through no willful action of her own, her intellectual property, her very costly bread and butter, fell into the hands of cybercriminals. We know that most companies—68 percent, according to data cited in Action Item #8—would choose not to increase their cybersecurity spend even after one of their vendors was breached. This suggests that many, if not most, companies also fail to evaluate the digital security and resilience of firms with which they regularly do business, even when they allow them to access their own networked systems via (as, for example, in the case of Target) estimating and billing programs. The fiduciary responsibilities of boards and C-level leadership do not end at the corporate network firewall.

Action Item #19

Never sacrifice business to security. "Air gapping" your business—pulling the plug on connectivity with the Internet—will dramatically increase your digital security. Unfortunately, the price is unacceptable. You go out of business. At the risk of repetition, remember: *security* is a security issue, not a business issue. When top leadership focuses exclusively on eliminating *security* risks, there is a high probability that its actions will make the business less efficient, less agile, less responsive, and therefore less profitable by heedlessly throttling access. Taking the wider view, a view that encompasses digital *resilience*—which *is* a business issue—compels the board and the C-suite to find, oversee, and audit solutions that balance network access with network restriction. Resilience is about enhancing profitability and value by prioritizing data assets and intelligently managing access to them for the purpose of business. Effective leaders resist the blind impulse to build walls. Instead, they demand that access be dynamically managed with vigilance informed by active intelligence and objective measurements.

Action Item #20

Get into the data loop. Top leadership needs to know what it knows and what it does not know. Look at how information on digital security and resilience is communicated to the top. Invite regular briefings from IT executives—CISO and CIO—to discuss the state of the organization's digital infrastructure, always bearing in mind that it is inherently dynamic and exists as one part of a much larger digital ecosystem.

Action Item #21

Give subject-matter experts a seat at the table. As boards typically include executives in compensation, audit, and other key functions, someone with a strong cybersecurity background should claim a seat at the boardroom table as well. Not every board member needs to be a cyber specialist, but all need sufficient understanding of their organization's networks to make informed decisions about risk and reward, risk and opportunity. All members should acquire sufficient training in network security to make IT-related evaluations and judgments aligned with their organization's risk appetite. The management of cyber-related risk should be integrated within the broader context of all other business risks. Consider forming dedicated committees to oversee and audit both cybersecurity and digital resilience throughout the enterprise. In addition to ensuring the availability of technical subject-matter experts, consider adding a special legal counsel experienced in data security issues.

Action Item #22

Get ready. The time to prepare for cyberattacks, which are inevitable, is now. In addition to auditing readiness and addressing any gaps that are found in readiness, reinforce your organization's culture of resilience (Action Item #12) by ensuring that it is, above all, a culture prepared for change. Whatever else a serious network breach is, it is *change*—sudden, radical, painful, scary, and potentially destabilizing. Ensure that you have people in place who are capable of nonroutine leadership and crisis management. Resilience is not just about resistance, it is also about recovery.

Action Item #23

Start playing games. Militaries play at wars much more than they fight real wars. This is not because they enjoy being soldiers, but because they understand that war entails all manner of uncertainty and the more you game out that uncertainty, the less uncertain it becomes. Top leadership needs to support digital wargames designed to hone resilience. This means finding out what works and what does not. It means challenging the status quo—existing procedures for breach response—and it means adopting and rehearsing whatever procedures appear to have the best prospect of prevailing in a crisis. As always, knowledge is essential to resilience. Gaming out a breach and your range of responses to it chips away at ignorance. All games have rules. Include among your rules everything you have decided about the balance between risk and opportunity, restriction of access and openness to the world.

Action Item #24

Act to reduce chaos. A serious network breach creates chaos. You cannot eliminate it. You cannot decree its suppression by executive fiat. You can, however, act to reduce it. Some of this reduction can come from good technology, but much of it requires top-down leadership that prepares and trains people at all levels in how to respond, how to behave, what to communicate, and what not to communicate in a digital crisis. A network breach is not an IT problem. It is a whole-business crisis that affects every employee and every stakeholder, including customers, partners, vendors, and investors. Top-down transparent, authoritative, and realistically affirmative communication is essential to rapid recovery. Ideally, resilience helps you avoid an attack or to quickly contain one. But when a breach results in substantial damage and data loss, resilience is essential to rapid and full recovery of business operations as well as stakeholder trust.

Action Item #25

Find the truth, hold onto the truth, present the truth. A network breach may be many things. It is, however, indisputably one thing: a crime—the ultimate cost of which can, to a significant degree, be managed, if the board and other top leadership act to gather, preserve, and present data. And since this is a crime, *data* is also *evidence.* In a cyber breach, top leadership has profound fiduciary responsibilities and potential exposure to criminal prosecution and civil action. Secure legal counsel, cooperate with government authorities and law enforcement, and conduct your own formal investigations—with the understanding that these will become part of the legal record. Prepare for a serious breach in advance by establishing procedures by which the CIO, CISO, and others are to communicate with designated top leadership, both internal and external counsel, and those with responsibility for investigations and compliance.

The primary goal of your investigation is to determine, first and foremost, whether the attackers remain in your network as a persistent threat. Are they still in the system? What malware have they left behind? Contain the damage. Stop the crime.

Beyond this, collect evidence to support a full investigation with the objective of learning from the breach: Who carried it out? Why? And how? Since knowledge is the key to resilience, learning from the breach will help make your enterprise more resilient.

Your investigation should not be aimed exclusively at minimizing your company's legal exposure, but should also be conducted with the objective of bringing action against the attacker in the form of criminal prosecution and pursuit of civil claims. Assess the liability of others, including vendors who may have failed to meet contractual obligations or may have carried them out in a negligent manner.

Action Item #26

Share your pain. After a breach, the natural impulse at the top is to hunker down and clam up. Resist this inclination. IBM's Caleb Barlow points out that most hackers remain forever anonymous and, therefore, remain forever beyond the reach of law enforcement. This being the case, he proposes changing "the economics for the bad guys" by making their crimes unprofitable. Barlow notes that the top priority in responding to a disease pandemic such as SARS, Ebola, bird flu, or Zika is "knowing who is infected and how the disease is spreading." In an outbreak, "governments, private institutions, hospitals, physicians" respond "openly and quickly" in "a collective and altruistic effort to stop the spread in its tracks and to inform anyone not infected how to protect or inoculate themselves." Although a cyberattack is in many ways similar to an infectious disease outbreak, organizations "are far more likely to keep information . . . to themselves." They are "worried about competitive advantage, litigation, or regulation."

Barlow wants "organizations to open up and share what is in their private arsenal of information." Sharing the information is "equivalent to inoculation. And if you're not sharing, you're actually part of the problem, because you're increasing the odds that other people could be impacted by the same attack techniques." Moreover, by detecting and stopping criminals' exploits "closer to real-time, we break their plans. We inform the people they aim to hurt far sooner than they had ever anticipated. We ruin their reputations, we crush their ratings and reviews. We make cybercrime not pay. We change the economics for the bad guys." With this objective in mind, IBM released more than "700 terabytes of actionable threat intelligence data, including information on real-time attacks that can be used to stop cybercrime in its tracks." As of December 2016, more than 4,000 organizations were "leveraging this data, including half of the Fortune 100." Barlow's hope is to "get all of those organizations to join [IBM] in the fight, and do the same thing and share their information on when and how they're being attacked."[20]

At the very least, in consultation with counsel and law enforcement, you need to share the news of an attack as well as the results of your investigation. The board and the C-suite should not hoard as privileged intellectual property the details of a breach and the lessons learned from it. Instead, this information should be regarded as knowledge to be shared freely with the business community. Your network exists in a digital ecosystem. Any knowledge with the potential to enhance the resilience of your network has the potential to make the ecosystem more resilient. The resilience of every network in the ecosystem enhances the resilience of yours.

TAKEAWAY

I admit it: I've written a long list of action steps leadership can take to become more resilient to the digital risks of our time. So, let me end with this single challenge to you. History is full of organizations and leaders who ignored the trends of the day, the evolving threats to their function and existence. Digital resilience does not happen overnight. In fact, resilience is a well-worn path through most physical aspects of our daily lives. Pause. Think about those experiences and requirements we put on ourselves in "real life" to make our world safer, more efficient, and less costly. Now, apply this thinking to your digital infrastructure, the one on which your business is so thoroughly dependent today. *That's* the single most urgent action step required.

Be a leader, change the way your company thinks about cyber, and I guarantee that you will be a leader who endures and is never surprised. When that big cyberattack hits your organization, you will be ready.

NOTES

CHAPTER 1

1. Mahesh Sharma, "FireEye Launches R&D Center in Bangalore" *ZDNet* (March 18, 2013), http://www.zdnet.com/article/fireeye-launches-r-d-center-in-bangalore/; Joel Christie, "Target Ignored High-Tech Security Sirens Warning Them of a Data Hack Operation BEFORE Cyber Criminals in Russia Made Off with 40 Million Stolen Credit Cards" *Daily Mail* (March 14, 2014), http://www.dailymail.co.uk/news/article-2581314/Target-ignored-high-tech-security-sirens-warning-data-hack-operation-BEFORE-cyber-criminals-Russia-40-million-stolen-credit-cards.html.

2. Ellen Nakashima, "U.S. Notified 3,000 Companies in 2013 about Cyberattacks" *The Washington Post* (March 24, 2014), https://www.washingtonpost.com/world/national-security/2014/03/24/74aff686-aed9-11e3-96dc-d6ea14c099f9_story.html?utm_term=.c7b28532c00c.

3. Ponemon Institute, http://www-01.ibm.com/common/ssi/cgi-bin/ssialias?htmlfid=SEL03094WWEN.

4. Andrew Zolli and Ann Marie Healy, *Resilience: Why Things Bounce Back* (New York: Free Press, 2012), 6, Kindle ed.

5. John Mulligan, "Written Testimony before the Senate Committee on Commerce, Science, and Transportation" (March 26, 2014), https://corporate.target.com/_media/TargetCorp/global/PDF/Target-SJC-032614.pdf.

6. Michael Riley, Benjamin Elgin, Dune Lawrence, and Carol Matlack, "Misses Alarms and 40 Million Stolen Credit Card Numbers: How Target Blew It" *Bloomberg* (March 17, 2014), http://www.bloomberg.com/news/articles/2014-03-13/target-missed-warnings-in-epic-hack-of-credit-card-data.

7. Mulligan, https://corporate.target.com/_media/TargetCorp/global/PDF/Target-SJC-032614.pdf.

8. Robert Hackett, "How Much Do Data Breaches Cost Big Companies? Shockingly Little" *Fortune* (March 27, 2015), http://fortune.

com/2015/03/27/how-much-do-data-breaches-actually-cost-big-companies-shockingly-little/.

9. Maggie McGrath, "Target Profit Falls 46% on Credit Card Breach and the Hits Could Keep on Coming" *Forbes* (February 26, 2014), http://www.forbes.com/sites/maggiemcgrath/2014/02/26/target-profit-falls-46-on-credit-card-breach-and-says-the-hits-could-keep-on-coming/.

10. Teri Radichel, *Case Study: Critical Controls That Could Have Prevented Target Breach* SANS Institute (August 5, 2014), 4, https://www.sans.org/reading-room/whitepapers/casestudies/case-study-critical-controls-prevented-target-breach-35412.

11. Jeff Williams, "9 Data Breaches That Cost Someone Their Job" *CSO from IDG* (December 16, 2014), http://www.csoonline.com/article/2859485/data-breach/9-data-breaches-that-cost-someone-their-job.html#slide2.

12. Radichel, 4, https://www.sans.org/reading-room/whitepapers/casestudies/case-study-critical-controls-prevented-target-breach-35412.

13. Mulligan, https://corporate.target.com/_media/TargetCorp/global/PDF/Target-SJC-032614.pdf.

14. Riley, Elgin, Lawrence, and Matlack, http://www.bloomberg.com/news/articles/2014-03-13/target-missed-warnings-in-epic-hack-of-credit-card-data.

15. Mandiant, "APT1: Exposing One of China's Cyber Espionage Units," https://www.fireeye.com/content/dam/fireeye-www/services/pdfs/mandiant-apt1-report.pdf.

16. Riley, Elgin, Lawrence, and Matlack, http://www.bloomberg.com/news/articles/2014-03-13/target-missed-warnings-in-epic-hack-of-credit-card-data.

17. Radichel, 2, https://www.sans.org/reading-room/whitepapers/casestudies/case-study-critical-controls-prevented-target-breach-35412; Aorato Labs, "The Untold Story of the Target Attack Step by Step" (August 2014), 4, https://aroundcyber.files.wordpress.com/2014/09/aorato-target-report.pdf.

18. Aorato Labs, https://aroundcyber.files.wordpress.com/2014/09/aorato-target-report.pdf; Radichel, https://www.sans.org/reading-room/whitepapers/casestudies/case-study-critical-controls-prevented-target-breach-35412.

19. SAP Ariba, http://www.ariba.com/help/ariba-answers/suppliers/billing-and-payment.

20. Target, "Becoming a Business Partner," https://vmm.partnersonline.com/vmm/register/becomeBusPartner.do.

21. Angry IP Scanner, http://angryip.org/.

22. Microsoft System Center, Orchestrator, https://technet.microsoft.com/en-us/library/hh237242(v=sc.12).aspx.

23. Margaret Rouse, "Kaptoxa," TechTarget, http://searchsecurity.techtarget.com/definition/Kaptoxa.

24. Krebs on Security, http://krebsonsecurity.com/tag/target-data-breach/page/2/; Cory Blair, "How an Independent Reporter Broke the Target Security Breach Story, and at What Risk" *American Journalism Review* (June 16, 2014), http://ajr.org/2014/06/16/reporter-mingles-criminals-cover-cybersecurity/.

25. Krebs on Security, "Cards Stolen in Target Breach Flood Underground Markets," http://krebsonsecurity.com/2013/12/cards-stolen-in-target-breach-flood-underground-markets/.

26. Riley, Elgin, Lawrence, and Matlack, http://www.bloomberg.com/news/articles/2014-03-13/target-missed-warnings-in-epic-hack-of-credit-card-data.

27. The literature on this is voluminous and growing. See *The New York Times* https://www.nytimes.com/news-event/russian-election-hacking.

28. Riley, Elgin, Lawrence, and Matlack, http://www.bloomberg.com/news/articles/2014-03-13/target-missed-warnings-in-epic-hack-of-credit-card-data.

29. Joshua Cooper Ramo, *The Seventh Sense: Power, Fortune, and Survival in the Age of Networks* New York: Little, Brown, 2016), 37 and 40.

30. Joel Christie, "Target Ignored High-Tech Security Sirens Warning Them of a Data Hack Operation BEFORE Cyber Criminals in Russia Made Off with 40 Million Stolen Credit Cards" *Daily Mail* (March 14, 2014), http://www.dailymail.co.uk/news/article-2581314/Target-ignored-high-tech-security-sirens-warning-data-hack-operation-BEFORE-cyber-criminals-Russia-40-million-stolen-credit-cards.html.

31. Andrew Zolli and Ann Marie Healy, *Resilience: Why Things Bounce Back* (New York: Free Press, 2012), 4–5, Kindle Ed.

32. Justin Wm. Moyer, Dana Hedgpeth, and Faiz Siddiqui, "Southwest Airlines Computer Glitch Causes Cancellations, Delays for Third Day" *The Washington Post* (July 22, 2016), https://www.washingtonpost.com/news/dr-gridlock/wp/2016/07/21/long-lines-for-southwest-airlines-passengers-at-area-airports/; Susan Carey, "Delta Meltdown Reflects Problems with Aging Technology"

The Wall Street Journal (August 8, 2016), http://www.wsj.com/articles/delta-air-lines-says-computers-down-everywhere-1470647527; Bradley Hope, "NYSE Says Wednesday Outage Caused by Software Update" *The Wall Street Journal* (July 10, 2015), http://www.wsj.com/articles/stocks-trade-on-nyse-at-open-1436450975; Jose Pagliery, "Tech Fail! Explaining Today's 3 Big Computer Errors" *CNN Money* (July 8, 2015), http://money.cnn.com/2015/07/08/technology/united-nyse-wsj-down/.

33. David E. Sanger and Nicole Perlroth, "U.S. Said to Find North Korea Ordered Cyberattack on Sony" *The New York Times* (December 17, 2014), http://www.nytimes.com/2014/12/18/world/asia/us-links-north-korea-to-sony-hacking.html?_r=3; IMDb, "*The Interview* (2014)," http://www.imdb.com/title/tt2788710/; Kim Zetter, "The Evidence That North Korea Hacked Sony Is Flimsy" *Wired* (December 17, 2014), https://www.wired.com/2014/12/evidence-of-north-korea-hack-is-thin/.

34. Greg Jaffe and Steven Mufson, "Obama Criticizes Sony's Decision to Pull 'The Interview'" *The Washington Post* (December 19, 2014), https://www.washingtonpost.com/politics/obama-criticizes-sonys-decision-to-pull-the-interview/2014/12/19/77d1ce9a-87ad-11e4-b9b7-b8632ae73d25_story.html.

35. WikiLeaks, "Search DNC Email Database," https://wikileaks.org/dnc-emails/.

36. Identity Theft Resource Center, "2016 Data Breach Category Summary" (August 9, 2016), http://www.idtheftcenter.org/images/breach/ITRCBreachStatsReportSummary2016.pdf.

37. Wade Williamson, "Data Breaches by the Numbers" *SecurityWeek* (August 31, 2015), http://www.securityweek.com/data-breaches-numbers.

38. Ponemon Institute, *2016 Cost of Data Breach Study: Global Analysis* (June 2016), http://www-01.ibm.com/common/ssi/cgi-bin/ssialias?htmlfid=SEL03094WWEN.

39. Zolli and Healy, 5.

40. Ibid.

41. Richard A. Clarke, *Cyber War: The Next Threat to National Security and What to Do About It* (New York: HarperCollins, 2010), 81.

42. Clarke, 83.

CHAPTER 2

1. CyberEdge Group, *2016 Cyberthreat Defense Report* Invincea, https://www.

invincea.com/wp-content/uploads/2016/03/CyberEdge-2016-CDR-infographic-Invincea-version.png.

2. IBM Security, *2016 Ponemon Cost of Data Breach Study* http://www-03.ibm.com/security/data-breach/.

3. UpGuard, "CISO's Guide to Cyber Resilience," https://www.upguard.com/ebooks/ciso-guide-to-cyber-resilience, 3.

4. Eugene Kapersky, "Kapersky Lab Investigates Hacker Attack on Its Own Network" *Kapersky Lab Daily* (June 10, 2015), https://blog.kaspersky.com/kaspersky-statement-duqu-attack/8997/; Kapersky Lab, "Duqu 2.0: Frequently Asked Questions," http://media.kaspersky.com/en/Duqu-2-0-Frequently-Asked-Questions.pdf. In 2017, allegations of Kaspersky Lab ties to the Russian government emerged; see Nicole Perroth and Scott Shane, "How Israel Caught Russian Hackers Scouring the World for U.S. Secrets," *The New York Times* (October 10, 2017), https://www.nytimes.com/2017/10/10/technology/kaspersky-lab-israel-russia-hacking.html?_r=0, and Shane Harris and Gordon Lubold, "Russia Has Turned Kaspersky Software Into Tool for Spying," *Wall Street Journal* (October 11, 2017), https://www.wsj.com/articles/russian-hackers-scanned-networks-world-wide-for-secret-u-s-data-1507743874. In September 2017, the United States government banned federal agencies from using Kaspersky Lab cybersecurity software; see Olivia Solon, "US government bans agencies from using Kaspersky software over spying fears," *The Guardian* (September 13, 2017), https://www.theguardian.com/technology/2017/sep/13/us-government-bans-kaspersky-lab-russian-spying.

5. GReAT, "The Mystery of Duqu 2.0: A Sophisticated Cyberespionage Actor Returns," SecureList (June 10, 2015), https://securelist.com/blog/research/70504/the-mystery-of-duqu-2-0-a-sophisticated-cyberespionage-actor-returns/.

6. Judith Rodin, *The Resilience Dividend: Being Strong in a World Where Things Go Wrong* (New York: Public Affairs, 1014), 4.

7. Rodin, 4.

8. Scott Hilton, "Dyn Analysis Summary of Friday October 21 Attack," Dyn Blog (October 26, 2016), http://hub.dyn.com/dyn-blog/dyn-analysis-summary-of-friday-october-21-attack.

9. Nicky Woolf, "DDoS Attack That Disrupted Internet Was Largest of Its Kind in History, Experts Say" *The Guardian* (October 26, 2016), https://www.theguardian.com/technology/2016/oct/26/ddos-attack-dyn-mirai-botnet.

10. Ibid.

11. Peter Lucas, Joe Ballay, and Mickey McManus, *Trillions: Thriving in the Emerging Information Economy* (Hoboken, NJ: John Wiley & Sons, 2012), xii.

12. Ibid.

13. Ibid.

14. Steve Mertl, "How Cars Have Become Rolling Computers" *The Globe and Mail* (March 5, 2016), http://www.theglobeandmail.com/globe-drive/how-cars-have-become-rolling-computers/article29008154/.

15. *PC Magazine Encyclopedia* "Definition of Tbps," http://www.pcmag.com/encyclopedia/term/64249/tbps.

16. Woolf, https://www.theguardian.com/technology/2016/oct/26/ddos-attack-dyn-mirai-botnet.

17. Joshua Cooper Ramo, *The Seventh Sense: Power, Fortune, and Survival in the Age of Networks* (New York: Little, Brown, 2016), 51, 52.

18. Ibid. 52.

19. Ibid. Melvin E. Conway, "How Do Committees Invent?" *Datamation* (April 1968), 31, http://www.melconway.com/Home/pdf/committees.pdf.

20. For an overview of the Tandem approach to digital resilience, see Joel Bartlett, Jim Gray, and Bob Horst, "Fault Tolerance in Tandem Computer Systems," Technical Report 86.2, Tandem Computers (March 1986), http://www.hpl.hp.com/techreports/tandem/TR-86.2.pdf.

21. Ramo, 53.

22. Natalie Gagliordi, "The Target Breach, Two Years Later," *ZDNet* (November 27, 2015), http://www.zdnet.com/article/the-target-breach-two-years-later/.

23. Andrew Zolli and Ann Marie Healy, *Resilience: Why Things Bounce Back* (New York: Free Press), 16; Kindle Ed.

24. Robert M. May, Simon A. Levin, and George Sugihara, "Ecology for Bankers," *Nature* vol. 451 (February 21, 2008), 893, http://www.people.wm.edu/~mdlama/courses/Nature-2008-May.pdf. The *Nature* article is a comment on a full-length report on the conference: J. Kambhu, S. Weidman, and N. Krishnan, (Washington, DC: National Academies Press, 2007), which was also published as *Economic Policy Review* 13(2), 2007.

25. Ibid.

26. Ibid.

27. Ibid.

28. Ibid. 893–894.

29. Ibid. 894.

30. Zolli and Healy, 11–12.

31. Ibid. 27.

32. Ibid. 13, 14.

33. Ibid. 22.

CHAPTER 3

1. Quoted in Joshua Cooper Ramo, *The Seventh Sense: Power, Fortune, and Survival in the Age of Networks* (New York: Little, Brown, 2016), 37.

2. Nicholas A. Christakis and James H. Fowler, *Connected: How Your Friends' Friends' Friends' Affect Everything You Feel, Think, and Do* (New York: Little, Brown, 2009), xvi.

3. Ewan Clayton, *The Golden Threat: The Story of Writing* (Berkeley, CA: Counterpoint, 2013), Chapter 1; Kindle ed.

4. The invention of the wheel certainly predates written history and therefore likely predates writing, with most authorities dating the wheel to the late Neolithic period (beginning around 10,200 BCE and ending between 4500 and 2000 BCE). The etymological precursor of the English-language word *wheel* seems to be Proto-Indo-European, which suggests that people had a word for an object we would recognize as the wheel by about 3500 BCE. See *Online Etymology Dictionary*, http://www.etymonline.com/index.php?term=wheel.

5. S. A. Murray, *The Library: An Illustrated History* (New York: Skyhorse Publishing), 17.

6. Roy McLeod, *The Library of Alexandria: Centre of Learning in the Ancient World* (London: I. B. Taurus, 20014), 70–74.

7. See "List of book-burning incidents," Wikipedia, https://en.wikipedia.org/wiki/List_of_book-burning_incidents#cite_note-188.

8. T. M. Gladstone, eyewitness account of the Sack of Lawrence, Kansas, http://www.eyewitnesstohistory.com/lawrencesack.htm.

9. Tom Wheeler, *Mr. Lincoln's T-Mails: The Untold Story of How Abraham Lincoln Used the Telegraph to Win the Civil War* (New York: HarperCollins, 2006), Introduction, Kindle ed.

10. *Lincoln* (2012), http://www.imdb.com/title/tt0443272/.

11. Tom Sandage, *The Victorian Internet: The Remarkable Story of the Telegraph and the Nineteenth Century's On-Line Pioneers* (Sandage, 1998). Sandage is science correspondent for *The Economist.*

12. A detailed account of this and the rest of Lincoln's perilous journey is found in Daniel Stashower, *The Hour of Peril: The Secret Plot to Murder Lincoln Before the Civil War* (New York: Minotaur Books, 2014).

13. International Cable Protection Committee, "Narrative History," https://www.iscpc.org/information/learn-about-submarine-cables/narrative-history/.

14. The account that follows is based on Paul Marks, "Dot-dash-diss: The Gentleman Hacker's 1903 Lulz" *NewScientist* (December 27, 2011), http://www.newscientist.com/article/mg21228440.700-dotdashdiss-the-gentleman-hackers-1903-lulz.html?full=true\#.VGoSxPmjPJ8.

15. Frierich L. Bauer, *Decrypted Secrets: Methods and Maxims of Cryptology* (Berlin and New York: Springer Verlag, 1997), 104–111.

16. The account that follows is based on "The History of Phone Phreaking," http://www.historyofphonephreaking.org/.

17. Nigel Linge, "How Steve Jobs and Steve Wozniak Started Their Career as Hackers" *LifeJacker* (April 1, 2014), http://www.lifehacker.com.au/2014/04/how-steve-jobs-and-steve-wozniak-started-their-career-as-hackers/; FiveThirtyEight, "Before They Created Apple, Jobs and Wozniak Hacked the Phone System," *FiveThirtyEight* (November 4, 2015), http://fivethirtyeight.com/features/before-they-created-apple-jobs-and-wozniak-hacked-the-phone-system/.

18. Philip Elmer-Dewitt, "Computers: The 414 Gang Strikes Again" *Time* (August 29, 1983), http://content.time.com/time/magazine/article/0,9171,949797,00.html; Associated Press, "Two Who Raided Computers Pleading Guilty" *The New York Times* (March 17, 1984), http://www.nytimes.com/1984/03/17/us/two-who-raided-computers-pleading-guilty.html; Associated Press, "Computer User Sentenced" *The New York Times* (May 1, 1984), http://www.nytimes.com/1984/05/01/us/computer-user-sentenced.html.

19. *WarGames* (1983), IMDb, http://www.imdb.com/title/tt0086567/.

20. See Kevin Mitnick, *Ghost in the Wires: My Adventures as the World's Most Wanted Hacker* (New York: Back Bay Books, 2012).

21. Maurice Possley and Laurie Cohen, "$70 Million Bank Theft Foiled," *Chicago Tribune* (May 19, 1988), http://articles.chicagotribune.com/1988-05-19/news/8803180387_1_chase-manhattan-bank-wire-transfers-sources.

22. For a contemporary account of the "Morris worm," see Bob Page, "A Report on the Internet Worm" (November 7, 1988), http://www.ee.ryerson.ca/~elf/hack/iworm.html.

23. Charles P. Pfleeger and Shari Lawrence Pfleeger, *Analyzing Computer Security: A Threat/Vulnerability/Countermeasure Approach* (Upper Saddle River, NJ: Prentice Hall Professional, 2011), sidebar 3-3, 87.

24. Ronald L. Rivest, "The Early Days of RSA—History and Lessons," ACM Turing Award Lecture, https://people.csail.mit.edu/rivest/pubs/ARS03.rivest-slides.pdf.

25. Glenn Hurowitz, "Show Me a 50-Foot Wall, and I'll Show You a 51-Foot Ladder" *Grist* (November 21, 2008), http://grist.org/article/napolitano-knows/.

26. Identity Theft Resource Center, "2016 Data Breach Category Summary," http://www.idtheftcenter.org/images/breach/ITRCBreachStatsReportSummary_2016.pdf.

27. Greg Saikin, "FBI Issues New Warning on Social Networking Risks" *Data Privacy Monitor* (June 6, 2012), https://www.dataprivacymonitor.com/online-privacy/fbi-issues-new-warning-on-social-networking-risks/.

28. Kevin Murnane, "How John Podesta's Emails Were Hacked and How to Prevent It from Happening to You," *Forbes* (October 21, 2016), http://www.forbes.com/sites/kevinmurnane/2016/10/21/how-john-podestas-emails-were-hacked-and-how-to-prevent-it-from-happening-to-you/#101ab7fd5c02, and Lisa Vaas, "DNC chief Podesta led to phishing link 'thanks to a typo,'" *Naked Security* (December 16, 2016), https://nakedsecurity.sophos.com/2016/12/16/dnc-chief-podesta-led-to-phishing-link-thanks-to-a-typo/.

29. Richard A. Clarke, *Cyber War: The Next Threat to National Security and What to Do About It* (New York: HarperCollins, 2010), 81.

30. The discussion that follows is drawn from Colin Delany, "How Social Media Accelerated Tunisia's Revolution: An Inside View," *epolitics.com* (February 10, 2011), http://www.epolitics.com/2011/02/10/how-social-media-accelerated-tunisias-revolution-an-inside-view/.

31. Nicole Hong, "Report Says Russian Hackers in DNC Breach Waged Wider Campaign" *Wall Street Journal* (June 26, 2016), http://www.wsj.com/articles/report-says-russian-hackers-in-dnc-breach-waged-wider-campaign-1466933401.
32. Ramo, 52.

CHAPTER 4

1. See "A History of Storage Cost," mkomo.com (September 8, 2009; updated 2014), http://www.mkomo.com/cost-per-gigabyte. Note that no manufacturer sold a storage device with a 1 gigabyte capacity in 1980; the cost is extrapolated from the cost of several devices capable of storing 5 to 26 megabytes.
2. Vannevar Bush, "As We May Think" *The Atlantic* (July 1945), available at http://www.theatlantic.com/magazine/archive/1945/07/as-we-may-think/303881/.
3. Tim Berners-Lee, "Answers for Young People," W3.org, https://www.w3.org/People/Berners-Lee/Kids.html.
4. Ibid.
5. For the sake of simplicity in this overview of digital networks, we will confine discussion to the four-layer TCP/IP model rather than the seven-layer OSI model. For those interested, however, note that the TCP/IP application layer includes the functions of the OSI application layer, presentation layer, and most of the session layer. The TCP/IP transport layer includes the "graceful close" function of the OSI session layer as well as the OSI transport layer. The TCP/IP internetwork layer corresponds to a subset of the OSI network layer. The TCP/IP link layer includes the OSI link layer and (sometimes) the OSI physical layers as well as some of the protocols of the OSI's network layers. In short, the two models, while different, do not conflict with each other.
6. Richard A. Clarke, *Cyber War: The Next Threat to National Security and What to Do About It* (New York: HarperCollins, 2010), 81.
7. Sewell Chan, "Giuliani, 9/11 and the Emergency Command Center, Continued" *The New York Times* (May 15, 2007), http://empirezone.blogs.nytimes.com/2007/05/15/giuliani-911-and-the-emergency-command-center-continued/?_r=0.
8. The "butterfly effect" was coined by Edward Norton Lawrence, one of the pioneering minds behind chaos theory, in "Predictability: Does the Flap of a Butterfly's Wings in Brazil Set Off a Tornado in Texas," a paper

presented at the 139th meeting of the American Association for the Advancement of Science on December 29, 1972, http://eaps4.mit.edu/research/Lorenz/Butterfly_1972.pdf.

CHAPTER 5

1. Per the U.S. Debt Clock, http://www.usdebtclock.org/cbo-omb-gop-budget-estimates.html.

2. "Grasping Large Numbers," The Endowment for Human Development, http://www.ehd.org/science_technology_largenumbers.php.

3. Peter Lucas, Joe Ballay, and Mickey McManus, *Trillions: Thriving in the Emerging Information Ecology* (Hoboken, NJ: John Wiley & Sons, 2012), xiv.

4. Lucas, Ballay, and McManus, 2, 3.

5. Ibid. 115, 117–118.

6. "Lockheed Martin's F-35 Lightning II Most Advanced Cockpit," *WordlessTech* https://wordlesstech.com/lockheed-martins-f-35-lightning-ii-most-advanced-cockpit/.

7. "The Glass Cockpit: Technology First Used in Military, Commercial Aircraft," NASA Langley Research Center (June 2000), https://www.nasa.gov/centers/langley/news/factsheets/Glasscockpit.html.

8. "Situational Awareness," SKYbrary, http://www.skybrary.aero/index.php/Situational_Awareness.

9. Peter Kotz, "Glass-Cockpit Blackout" *Plane & Pilot* (October 21, 2008), http://www.planeandpilotmag.com/article/glass-cockpit-blackout/#.WEGtD_ArIuU.

10. See, for example, John Zimmerman, "The Great Debate: Are Glass Cockpits Better?" *Air Facts* (January 3, 2012), http://airfactsjournal.com/2012/01/the-great-debate-are-glass-cockpits-better/; John P. Young, Richard O. Fanjoy, and Michael W. Suckow, "Impact of Glass Cockpit Experience on Manual Flight Skills" *Journal of Aviation/Aerospace Education & Research* (Winter 2006), 15:2, article 5, http://commons.erau.edu/cgi/viewcontent.cgi?article=1501&context=jaaer; Mike Danko, "NTSB: Glass Cockpits Associated with Higher Rate of Fatal Accidents" *Aviation Law Monitor* (March 13, 2010), http://www.aviationlawmonitor.com/2010/03/articles/general-aviation/ntsb-glass-cockpits-associated-with-higher-rate-of-fatal-accidents/.

11. Reuters, "U.S. Customs Computer Outage Causes Delays at Some

Airports" (January 3, 2017), http://www.reuters.com/article/us-usa-immigration-customs-idUSKBN14N04H.

12. Lucas, Ballay, and McManus, 63.

13. Ibid.

14. Ibid. 64.

15. Koshu Nishiyama Hot Spring website, http://www.keiunkan.co.jp/en/; Chris Morris, "The World's Oldest Hotel Has Been a Family Business for 1,200 Years" *Fortune* (January 26, 2016), http://fortune.com/2016/01/26/oldest-hotel-keiunkan/.

16. Kim Gittleson, "Can a Company Live Forever?," *BBC News* (January 19, 2012), http://www.bbc.com/news/business-16611040.

17. Arie de Geus, *The Living Company: Habits for Survival in a Turbulent Business Environment* (Boston: Harvard Business School Press, 2002), 1.

18. Lucas, Ballay, and McManus, 70.

19. Ibid.

20. Ibid.136–137.

21. Ibid. 212.

22. Tom Simonite, "The Seemingly Unfixable Crack in the Internet's Backbone" *MIT Technology Review* (August 6, 2015), https://www.technologyreview.com/s/540056/the-seemingly-unfixable-crack-in-the-internets-backbone/.

23. Risk may be defined as the probability of an incident times the consequence of an incident. A nuclear weapons accident has a low chance of occurrence, but a high impact. The same is true of serious commercial airline accidents. They are rare, but their consequence is often a mass causality. An incident that disables the BGP may be rare, but its consequence could be the takedown of a major portion of the Internet.

24. Simonite, https://www.technologyreview.com/s/540056/the-seemingly-unfixable-crack-in-the-internets-backbone/.

25. Jim Cowie, "The New Threat: Targeted Internet Traffic Misdirection," Dyn Research (November 19, 2013), http://research.dyn.com/2013/11/mitm-internet-hijacking/.

26. Simonite, https://www.technologyreview.com/s/540056/the-seemingly-unfixable-crack-in-the-internets-backbone/.

27. David E. Sanger and Eric Schmitt, "Russian Ships Near Data Cables Are

Too Close for U.S. Comfort" *The New York Times* (October 25, 2015), http://www.nytimes.com/2015/10/26/world/europe/russian-presence-near-undersea-cables-concerns-us.html?_r=0.

28. Ian Traynor, "Russia Accused of Unleashing Cyberwar to Disable Estonia" *The Guardian* (May 16, 2007), https://www.theguardian.com/world/2007/may/17/topstories3.russia.

29. Jeffrey Carr, *Inside Cyber Warfare* (N.p.: O'Reilly Media, 2011), Kindle Edition, chap. 7. The organization has been implicated not only in the cyberattacks against Estonia, but also in internal Russian government operations. A February 6, 2009 *Moscow Times* article revealed, "Anna Bukovskaya, a St. Petersburg activist with the pro-Kremlin Nashi youth group, said she coordinated a group of 30 young people who infiltrated branches" of several "banned" political parties and organizations "in Moscow, St. Petersburg, Voronezh, and six other cities," for which she was paid 40,000 rubles per month by the government (Carr, chap. 7).

30. John Markoff, "Before the Gunfire, Cyberattacks" *The New York Times* (August 12, 2008), http://www.nytimes.com/2008/08/13/technology/13cyber.html.

31. Greg Miller, "Undersea Internet Cables Are Surprisingly Vulnerable" *Wired* (October 29, 2015), https://www.wired.com/2015/10/undersea-cable-maps/.

32. Pelton was tried, convicted, and sentenced to life imprisonment for his espionage. Matthew Carle, "Operation Ivy Bells," *Military.com Remembers the Cold War*, http://www.military.com/Content/MoreContent1/?file=cw_f_ivybells.

33. Glenn Greenwald, "NSA Prism Program Taps in to User Data of Apple, Google and Others" *The Guardian* (June 7, 2013), https://www.theguardian.com/world/2013/jun/06/us-tech-giants-nsa-data; Barton Gellman and Laura Poitras, "U.S., British Intelligence Mining Data from Nine U.S. Internet Companies in Broad Secret Program" *Washington Post* (June 7, 2013), https://www.washingtonpost.com/investigations/us-intelligence-mining-data-from-nine-us-internet-companies-in-broad-secret-program/2013/06/06/3a0c0da8-cebf-11e2-8845-d970ccb04497_story.html?utm_term=.b6f45edcf604.

34. http://www.theatlantic.com/international/archive/2013/07/the-creepy-long-standing-practice-of-undersea-cable-tapping/277855/.

35. http://www.nytimes.com/2005/02/20/politics/new-nuclear-sub-is-said-to-have-special-eavesdropping-ability.html.

36. Fabian Schmidt, "Tapping the World's Fiber Optic Cables," *Deutsche Welle* (June 30, 2013), http://www.dw.com/en/tapping-the-worlds-fiber-optic-cables/a-16916476.

37. http://www.theatlantic.com/international/archive/2013/07/the-creepy-long-standing-practice-of-undersea-cable-tapping/277855/.

38. Nicky Woolf, "DDoS Attack That Disrupted Internet Was Largest of Its Kind in History, Experts Say" *The Guardian* (October 26, 2016), https://www.theguardian.com/technology/2016/oct/26/ddos-attack-dyn-mirai-botnet.

39. Matt Hamblen, "DDoS Attack Shows Dangers of IoT 'Running Rampant,'" *ComputerWorld* (October 25, 2016), http://www.computerworld.com/article/3135285/security/ddos-attack-shows-dangers-of-iot-running-rampant.html.

40. Thomas C. Reed, *At the Abyss: An Insider's History of the Cold War* (New York: Ballantine Books, 2004), Kindle Edition, chap. 17. Also see Gus W. Weiss, "The Farewell Dossier: Duping the Soviets," Central Intelligence Agency, https://www.cia.gov/library/center-for-the-study-of-intelligence/csi-publications/csi-studies/studies/96unclass/farewell.htm. In some circles, this document has raised doubts about Reed's account, because it reports that the CIA was involved in the installation of "flawed turbines . . . on a [Soviet] gas pipeline," but makes no mention of sabotaged SCADA software, nor does it even note that the flawed turbines were the cause of an explosion.

41. Fred Schreier, *On Cyberwarfare* DCAF Horizon 2015 Working Paper No. 7 (Geneva: Geneva Centre for the Democratic Control of Armed Forces, 2012), 107–108; Johnny Ryan, "iWar: A New Threat, Its Convenience—and Our Increasing Vulnerability," Winter 2007.

42. Clay Wilson, *Botnets, Cybercrime, and Cyberterrorism: Vulnerabilities and Policy Issues for Congress*, Congressional Research Service Report for Congress, January 29, 2008, 7–8.

43. Euan McKirdy and Mary Ilyushina, "Putin: 'Patriotic' Russian Hackers May Have Targeted U.S. Election," *CNN Politics* (June 2, 2017), http://www.cnn.com/2017/06/01/politics/russia-putin-hackers-election/index.html.

44. Sarwar A. Kashmeri, *NATO 2.0: Reboot or Delete?* (Washington, D.C.: Potomac Books, 2011), 51–52.

45. David Corn, "The NSA Chief Says Russia Hacked the 2016 Election.

Congress Must Investigate" *Mother Jones* (November 16, 2016), http://www.motherjones.com/politics/2016/11/will-congress-investigate-russian-interference-2016-campaign; Elizabeth Gurdus, "We're Headed for a 'Cyber Pearl Harbor,' Says Adm James Stavridis," *CNBC* (December 15, 2016), http://www.cnbc.com/2016/12/15/were-headed-at-a-cyber-pearl-harbor-says-adm-james-stavridis.html.

CHAPTER 6

1. Herman Melville, *Moby-Dick, or The Whale* (1851), chap. 72.

2. Evan Hansen, "Manning-Lamo Chat Logs Revealed" *Wired* (July 13, 2011), https://www.wired.com/2011/07/manning-lamo-logs/.

3. BBC News, "Chelsea Manning: Wikileaks Source Celebrates 'First Steps of Freedom,'" *BBC News* (May 17, 2017), http://www.bbc.com/news/world-us-canada-39947602.

4. Bob Dylan, "Subterranean Homesick Blues," Bob Dylan website, http://bobdylan.com/songs/subterranean-homesick-blues/.

5. Kelly Dickerson, "12 Ways Matt Damon Uses Science to Survive in 'The Martian,'" *Business Insider* (September 16, 2015), http://www.businessinsider.com/science-the-shit-out-of-mars-the-martian-2015-9. "I'm going to have to science the shit out of this" has become an Internet meme. Neil deGrasse Tyson, astrophysicist and director of the Hayden Planetarium, has even tweeted it as his favorite line out of the movie (https://twitter.com/neiltyson/status/610997574808395777?lang=en), and, if you are nerd enough, you can buy any number of T-shirts emblazoned with the phrase. Just google it.

6. "How My FICO Scores Are Calculated," *myFICO*, http://www.myfico.com/credit-education/whats-in-your-credit-score/.

7. Vindu Goel and Michael J. de la Merced, "Yahoo's Sale to Verizon Ends an Era for a Web Pioneer" *The New York Times* (July 24, 2016), http://www.nytimes.com/2016/07/25/business/yahoo-sale.html.

8. Nicole Perlroth, "Yahoo Says Hackers Stole Data on 500 Million Users in 2014" *The New York Times* (September 22, 2016), http://www.nytimes.com/2016/09/23/technology/yahoo-hackers.html.

9. Vindu Goel and Nicole Perlroth, "Yahoo Says 1 Billion User Accounts Were Hacked" *The New York Times* (December 14, 2016), http://www.nytimes.com/2016/12/14/technology/yahoo-hack.html.

10. Pau Szoldra, "The Dark Web Marketplace Where You Can Buy

200 Million Yahoo Accounts Is Under Cyberattack" *Business Insider* (September 22, 2016), http://www.businessinsider.com/real-deal-market-ddos-2016-9?r=DE&IR=T.

11. Vindu Goel and Nicole Perlroth, "Hacked Yahoo Data Is for Sale on Dark Web" *The New York Times* (December 15, 2016), http://www.nytimes.com/2016/12/15/technology/hacked-yahoo-data-for-sale-dark-web.html.

12. Scott Moritz and Brian Womack, "Verizon Explores Lower Price or Even Exit from Yahoo Deal" *Bloomberg Technology* (December 15, 2016), https://www.bloomberg.com/news/articles/2016-12-15/verizon-weighs-scrapping-yahoo-deal-on-hacking-liability; Reuters, "Yahoo Shareholders Approve $4.48B Merger with Verizon" *New York Post* (June 8, 2017), http://nypost.com/2017/06/08/yahoo-shareholders-approve-4-48b-merger-with–verizon/; Vindu Goel, "Verizon Completes $4.48 Billion Purchase of Yahoo, Ending an Era," *The New York Times* (June 13, 2017), https://www.nytimes.com/2017/06/13/technology/yahoo-verizon-marissa-mayer.html?_r=0.

13. Thomas L. Friedman, *The World Is Flat: A Brief History of the Twenty-first Century* (New York: Farrar, Straus and Giroux, 2005).

CHAPTER 7

1. "Planck Mission Brings Universe into Sharp Focus," *NASA News* (March 21, 2013), https://www.nasa.gov/mission_pages/planck/news/planck20130321.html; "Dark Energy, Dark Matter," *NASA Science Beta*, https://science.nasa.gov/astrophysics/focus-areas/what-is-dark-energy/.

2. James M. Kaplan, Tucker Bailey, Derek O'Halloran, Alan Marcus, and Chris Rezek, *Beyond Cybersecurity: Protecting Your Digital Business* (Hoboken, NJ: Wiley, 2015), xxiii.

3. Ibid.

4. Ibid.

5. Ibid.

6. See Kaplan et al., xxiv–xxvi. Only material enclosed in quotations is directly quoted from this source.

7. Kaplan et al., 160–161.

8. A February 26, 2015, FCC ruling favored net neutrality (see Jose Pagliery, "FCC Adopts Historic Internet Rules," *CNN Tech* [February

26, 2015], http://money.cnn.com/2015/02/26/technology/fcc-rules-net-neutrality/), but on May 18, 2017, the FCC voted to roll back net neutrality regulations (see Brian Fung, "The Future of Net Neutrality in Trump's America" *Washington Post* [April 5, 2016], https://www.washingtonpost.com/news/the-switch/wp/2017/04/05/the-future-of-net-neutrality-in-trumps-america/?utm_term=.97de3a87890c; Paige Agostin, "Trump's FCC Chief Is Right to Roll Back Net Neutrality Rule" *The Hill* [May 5, 2017], http://thehill.com/blogs/pundits-blog/technology/332099-ajit-pais-fcc-is-right-to-roll-back-the-regulatory-overreach-of; Alina Selyukh, "FCC Votes to Begin Rollback of Net Neutrality Regulations" *The Two-Way: Breaking News from NPR* [May 18, 2017], http://www.npr.org/sections/thetwo-way/2017/05/18/528941897/fcc-votes-to-begin-rollback-of-net-neutrality-regulations).

9. Henrik Andersson, James Kaplan, and Brent Smolinski, "Capturing Value from IT Infrastructure Innovation," *McKinsey & Company/Digital McKinsey* (October 2012), http://www.mckinsey.com/business-functions/digital-mckinsey/our-insights/capturing-value-from-it-infrastructure-innovation.

10. Kaplan et al., 103.

11. Peter Lucas, Joe Ballay, and Mickey McManus, *Trillions: Thriving in the Emerging Information Ecology* (Hoboken, NJ: John Wiley & Sons, 2012), 69.

12. The SSAE 16 Guide, http://www.ssae16guide.com/; CSA (Cloud Security Alliance), https://cloudsecurityalliance.org/#.

13. Information Security Forum, *Threat Horizon 2018: Lost in a Maze of Uncertainty* https://www.securityforum.org/research/threat-horizon-2e-of-uncertainty/.

14. Ibid.

15. Ibid.

16. Ibid.

17. Ibid.

18. Ibid.

19. Kaplan et al., 192–193.

20. Staff, "The COE International Convention on Cybercrime Before Its Entry into Force" *Copyright Bulletin* (January-March 2004), http://portal.unesco.org/culture/en/ev.php-URL_ID=19556&URL_DO=DO_TOPIC&URL_SECTION=201.html; Council of Europe, "Chart of

Signatures and Ratifications of Treaty 185," http://www.coe.int/en/web/conventions/full-list/-/conventions/treaty/185/signatures.

21. Council of Europe, "Convention on Cybercrime," Preamble, opened for signature November 23, 2001, C.E.T.S. No. 185.

22. Jack Goldsmith, "Cybersecurity Treaties: A Skeptical View," *Hoover Institution* (2011), 3, http://media.hoover.org/sites/default/files/documents/FutureChallenges_Goldsmith.pdf.

23. Goldsmith, 3–4.

CHAPTER 8

1. See Edwin E. Ghiselli and Jacob P. Siegel, "Leadership and Managerial Success in Tall and Flat Organization Structures," *Personnel Psychology,* vol. 25, no. 4 (December 1972), 617–624.

2. Vivian Giang, "What Kind of Leadership Is Needed in Flat Hierarchies?," *Fast Company* (May 19, 2015), https://www.fastcompany.com/3046371/what-kind-of-leadership-is-needed-in-flat-hierarchies.

3. Giang, https://www.fastcompany.com/3046371/what-kind-of-leadership-is-needed-in-flat-hierarchies.

4. Eric Dezenhall, "A Look Back the Target Breach," *The Huffington Post* (June 6, 2015), http://www.huffingtonpost.com/eric-dezenhall/a-look-back-at-the-target_b_7000816.html, and Kevin M. McGinty, "Target Breach Price Tag: #252 Million and Counting," *MintzLevin Privacy and Security Matters* (February 26, 2015), https://www.privacyandsecuritymatters.com/2015/02/target-data-breach-price-tag-252-million-and-counting/.

5. Craig Newman, "Lessons from the War over the Target Data Breach," *NACD Blog* (July 27, 2016), https://blog.nacdonline.org/2016/07/lessons-from-the-war-over-the-target-data-breach/.

6. Dana Post, "Cybersecurity in the Boardroom: The New Reality for Directors," *The Privacy Advisor* (May 27, 2014), https://iapp.org/news/a/cybersecurity-in-the-boardroom-the-new-reality-for-directors/.

7. "Why Everything Is Hackable," *The Economist* (April 8, 2017), 69–71.

8. Ibid. 69.

9. Caleb Barlow, "Where Is Cybercrime Really Coming From?," TED@IBM (November 2016), https://www.ted.com/talks/caleb_barlow_where_is_cybercrime_really_coming_from?language=en.

10. Ibid.
11. "Why Everything is Hackable," 69.
12. Ibid.
13. Ibid. 71.
14. Robert S. Mueller, III, Remarks to RSA Cyber Security Conference, San Francisco, March 1, 2012, https://archives.fbi.gov/archives/news/speeches/combating-threats-in-the-cyber-world-outsmarting-terrorists-hackers-and-spies.
15. NACD Online, "Dr. Phyllis A. Schneck, Keynote Cybersecurity," *YouTube* (September 20, 1016), https://www.youtube.com/watch?v=I-yIPGpwu1k.
16. EY, "Path to Cyber Resilience: Sense, Resist, React: EY's 19th Global Information Security Survey 2016–17," 9.
17. Ibid. 10.
18. Nicole Perlroth, "Hackers Find Celebrities' Weak Links in Their Vendor Chains" *The New York Times* (May 7, 2017), https://www.nytimes.com/2017/05/07/technology/hackers-exploit-celebrities-vendor-chains.html?_r=0.
19. Krebs on Security, "Email Attack on Vendor Set Up Breach at Target," February 2014, https://krebsonsecurity.com/2014/02/email-attack-on-vendor-set-up-breach-at-target/.
20. Barlow, https://www.ted.com/talks/caleb_barlow_where_is_cybercrime_really_coming_from?language=en.

INDEX

INDEX

INDEX

INDEX

INDEX